Natural Language Processing for Translation Memories 2015 (NLP4TM 2015)

International Conference on Recent Advances in Natural Language Processing 2015

Hissar, Bulgaria
11 September 2015

ISBN: 978-1-5108-1786-9

Printed from e-media with permission by:

Curran Associates, Inc.
57 Morehouse Lane
Red Hook, NY 12571

Some format issues inherent in the e-media version may also appear in this print version.

Printed by Curran Associates, Inc. (2015)

For permission requests, please contact the Association for Computational Linguistics at the address below.

Association for Computational Linguistics
209 N. Eighth Street
Stroudsburg, Pennsylvania 18360

Phone: 1-570-476-8006
Fax: 1-570-476-0860

acl@aclweb.org

Additional copies of this publication are available from:

Curran Associates, Inc.
57 Morehouse Lane
Red Hook, NY 12571 USA
Phone: 845-758-0400
Fax: 845-758-2634
Email: curran@proceedings.com
Web: www.proceedings.com

Introduction

Translation Memories (TM) are amongst the most used tools by professional translators. The underlying idea of TMs is that a translator should benefit as much as possible from previous translations by being able to retrieve how a similar sentence was translated before. Despite the fact that the core idea of these systems relies on comparing segments (typically of sentence length) from the document to be translated with segments from previous translations, most of the existing TM systems hardly use any language processing for this. Instead of addressing this issue, most of the work on translation memories focused on improving the user experience by allowing processing of a variety of document formats, intuitive user interfaces, and so on.

The term second generation translation memories has been around for more than ten years and it promises translation memory software that integrates linguistic processing in order to improve the translation process. This linguistic processing can involve the matching of subsentential chunks, the editing of distance operations between syntactic trees, and the incorporation of semantic and discourse information in the matching process. Terminologies, glossaries and ontologies are also very useful for translation memories, facilitating the task of the translator and ensuring a consistent translation. The field of Natural Language Processing (NLP) has proposed numerous methods for terminology extraction and ontology extraction which can be integrated in the translation process. The building of translation memories from corpora is another field where methods from NLP can contribute to improving the translation process.

We are happy we could include in the workshop programme 4 long contributions and 3 short papers dealing with the aforementioned issues.

Vít Baisa, Aleš Horák and Marek Medved' discuss in *Increasing Coverage of Translation Memories with Linguistically Motivated Segment Combination Methods* how it is possible to extend existing translation memories using linguistically motivated segments combining approaches concentrated on preserving high translational quality.

Linked to the topic of enhancing existing translation memories, in the paper *Spotting false translation segments in translation memories* Eduard Barbu presents a method for identifying false translations in translation memories thought as a classification task.

In *Improving translation memory fuzzy matching by paraphrasing*, Konstantinos Chatzitheodorou explores the use of paraphrasing in retrieving better segments from translation memories. The method relies on NooJ and performs consistently better than the state of the art on EN-IT language pair.

CATaLog: New Approaches to TM and Post Editing Interfaces presents a new CAT tool by Tapas Nayek, Sudip Kumar Naskar, Santanu Pal, Marcos Zampieri, Mihaela Vela and Josef van Genabith. The aim of the tool is to improve both the performance and the productivity of post-editing.

Carla Parra Escartín aims at bridging the gap between academic research on Translation Memories (TMs) and the actual needs and wishes of translators in *Creation of new TM segments: Fulfilling translators' wishes*. She presents a pilot study where the requests of translators are being implemented in the translation workflow.

Katerina Timonera and Ruslan Mitkov explore the use of clause splitting in better retrieval of segments. Their paper *Improving Translation Memory Matching through Clause Splitting* show that their method leads to a statistically significant increase in the number of retrieved matches when both the input segments and the segments in the TM are first processed with a clause splitter.

The Organising Committee would like to thank the Programme Committee, who responded with very fast but also substantial reviews for the workshop programme. This workshop would not have been possible without the support received from the EXPERT project (FP7/2007-2013 under REA grant agreement no. 317471, http://expert-itn.eu).

Constantin Orăsan and Rohit Gupta

Organizers:

Constantin Orăsan, University of Wolverhampton, UK

Rohit Gupta, University of Wolverhampton, UK

Program Committee:

Manuel Arcedillo, Hermes, Spain
Juanjo Arevalillo, Hermes, Spain
Eduard Barbu, Translated, Italy
Yves Champollion, WordFast, France
Gloria Corpas, University of Malaga, Spain
Maud Ehrmann, EPFL, Switzerland
Kevin Flanagan, Swansea University, UK
Gabriela Gonzalez, eTrad, Argentina
Manuel Herranz, Pangeanic, Spain
Qun Liu, DCU, Ireland
Ruslan Mitkov, University of Wolverhampton, UK
Gabor Proszeky, Morphologic, Hungary
Uwe Reinke, Cologne University of Applied Sciences, Germany
Michel Simard, NRC, Canada
Mark Shuttleworth, UCL, UK
Masao Utiyama, NICT, Japan
Andy Way, DCU, Ireland
Marcos Zampieri, Saarland University and DFKI, Germany
Ventsislav Zhechev, Autodesk

Invited Speaker:

Marcello Federico, Fondazione Bruno Kessler, Italy

Table of Contents

Conference Program

9:00–9:10 *Welcome*
Constantin Orasan

9:10–10:10 *Automatically tidying up and extending translation memories (invited talk)*
Marcello Federico, FBK, Italy

10:15–11:00 *Creation of new TM segments: Fulfilling translators' wishes*
Carla Parra Escartín

11:30–12:15 *Spotting false translation segments in translation memories*
Eduard Barbu

12:15–13:00 *Improving Translation Memory Matching through Clause Splitting*
Katerina Raisa Timonera and Ruslan Mitkov

14:30–15:00 *Improving translation memory fuzzy matching by paraphrasing*
Konstantinos Chatzitheodoroou

15:00–15:30 *Increasing Coverage of Translation Memories with Linguistically Motivated Segment Combination Methods*·
Vít Baisa, Ales Horak and Marek Medved'

15:30–16:00 *CATaLog: New Approaches to TM and Post Editing Interfaces*
Tapas Nayek, Sudip Kumar Naskar, Santanu Pal, Marcos Zampieri, Mihaela Vela and Josef van Genabith

16:15–17:00 ***Round table and final discussion***

Creation of new TM segments: Fulfilling translators' wishes

Carla Parra Escartín
Hermes Traducciones
C/ Cólquide 6, portal 2, 3.ž I
28230 Las Rozas, Madrid, Spain
carla.parra@hermestrans.com

Abstract

This paper aims at bridging the gap between academic research on Translation Memories (TMs) and the actual needs and wishes of translators. Starting from an internal survey in a translation company, we analyse what translators wished translation memories offered them. We are currently implementing one of their suggestions to assess its feasibility and whether or not it retrieves more TM matches as originally expected. We report on how the suggestion is being implemented, and the results obtained in a pilot study.

1 Introduction

Professional translators use translation memories on a daily basis. In fact, most translation projects nowadays require the usage of Computer Assisted Translation (CAT) tools. Sometimes translators will freely choose to work with a particular tool, and sometimes it will be the client who imposes the usage of such tool. One of the main advantages of CAT tools is that they allow for the integration of different productivity enhancement features.

Translation Memories (TMs) are used to retrieve past translations and partial past translations (fuzzy matches). Terminology databases (TBs) are used to enhance the coherence on terminology and to ensure that the right terminology is used in all projects. Moreover, some CAT tools offer additional functionalities such as the usage of predictive texts ("Autosuggest" in SDL Trados Studio[1] and "Muses" in MemoQ[2]), the automatic assembly of fragments to produce translations of new segments, or specific, customizable, Quality Assurance (QA) features.

[1] www.sdl.com
[2] www.memoq.com

In the context of a translation company, the usage of these productivity enhacement tools is part of the whole translation workflow. Project managers use them to generate word counts and estimate the time and resources needed to make the translation. They also use them to pre-translate files and clean them up prior to delivery to the client. Translators use these tools to translate, revise and proofread the translations prior to final delivery.

Several researchers have worked on enhancing TMs using Natural Language Processing (NLP) techniques (Hodász and Pohl, 2005; Pekar and Mitkov, 2007; Mitkov and Corpas, 2008; Simard and Fujita, 2012; Gupta and Orăsan, 2014; Vanallemeersch and Vandeghinste, 2015; Gupta et al., 2015). Despite reporting positive results, it seems that the gap between academic research and industry still exists. We carried out an internal survey in our company to detect potential new features for TMs that could be implemented by our R&D team. The aim was to identify potential new features that project managers and translators wished for and that would enhance their productivity. In this paper, we report on the results of that survey and further explain how we are implementing one of the suggestions we received. The remainder of this paper is structured as follows: Section 3 summarises the survey we carried out and the replies we got and our company is briefly introduced in Section 2. Section 4 explains how we implemented one of the suggestions we received. Subsections 4.1–4.3 describe how we created new TM segments out of existing TMs. Section 5 reports on the evaluation on a pilot test to assess the real usability of this approach. Finally, section 6 summarises our work and discusses future work.

2 Our company

Hermes is a leader company in the translation industry in Spain. It was founded in 1991 and has

Proceedings of the Workshop on Natural Language Processing for Translation Memories (NLP4TM), pages 1–8,
Hissar, Bulgaria, Sept 2015.

a vast experience in multilingual localisation and translation projects. With offices in Madrid and Málaga, the company has broad knowledge and experience in computer-assisted translation software and specific localisation software, including SDL Trados, memoQ, Déjà Vu, IBM TranslationManager, Star Transit, WordFast, Catalyst, Passolo, Across, Idiom World Server, Microsoft Helium and Microsoft Localisation Studio, among others.

Our company objectives are built upon a solid foundation which have allowed us to achieve a double quality certification for translation services (UNE-EN-15038:2006 and ISO-9001:2008 standards). Our in-house translators and project managers commit daily to provide our clients with high quality translations for different specialised fields (IT, medicine, technical manuals, general texts, etc.).

3 Internal survey

We asked our in-house translators and project managers for potential new functionalities that CAT tools could offer them. More concretely, we asked them which was, according to them, the "missing functionality" as far as TMs are concerned. In total, 10 project manager and 14 translators participated in this internal survey. While not all had a clear idea of what could be implemented, some interesting suggestions came up.

We gathered ideas such as scheduling automatic TM reorganisation to prevent that large TMs end up corrupted. It is a well known fact that large TMs need to be periodically reorganized (i.e. re-indexed and eventually cleaned-up). While this feature is available in standard CAT tools such as Studio 2014[3] and memoQ[4], it is not always carried out automatically and it is difficult to estimate when such reorganisation should be carried out. Scheduling it to be run automatically when a particular number of segments (e.g. 500) have been added since the last reorganisation, for instance, would prevent the loss of a TM because of bad maintenance.

Ideas more related to NLP included the automatic correction of orthotypography in the target language, and allowing for multilingual TMs where several source and target languages can be used for concordance searches at once. Although currently it is possible to use multilingual TMs in CAT tools, when starting a new project a language pair has to be selected. This leads to an underusage of the TM, and the potential benefits of querying multiple languages at once are missed. If, for instance, the TM contains a translation unit (TU) for a different pair of languages (e.g. German > Italian) than the ones selected for that specific project (e.g. German > French) and the same source sentence is appearing in the text currently being translated, the translation into a different target language will not be shown (i.e. the Italian translation of the German TU will not be matched). The same would occur with concordance searches. While matches for a different language pair will not be used in the translation, they may be useful for carrying it out. If a translator understands other target languages, these translations may give them a hint as to how to translate the same sentence into their mother tongue[5].

Finally, an interesting idea was to generate new segments on the fly from fragments of previously translated segments. Flanagan (2015) offers an interesting overview about the techniques used by different CAT tools for subsegment matching. Here, we will focus on memoQ's such functionality: "fragment assembly"[6].

Figure 1 shows how this functionality works in memoQ. As may be observed, memoQ looks

[3]In previous versions of Studio, TM reorganisation was available for all types of TMs in the "Translation Memory Settings Dialog Box > Performance and Tuning". As of Studio 2014, file-based TMs are automatically reorganised, while server-based TMs require periodical reorganisation. For further information, see: http://producthelp.sdl.com/SDL\%20Trados\%20Studio/client_en/Ref/O-T/TM_Settings/Translation_Memory_Settings_Dialog_Box__Performance_and_Tuning.htm

[4]memoQ actually has a repairing function, the "Translation memory repair wizard", which aims at repairing (i.e. re-indexing) a corrupted TM. According to the documentation, it is also possible to run this function on TMs which are not corrupted. For further information, see: http://kilgray.com/memoq/2015/help-en/index.html?repair_resource3.html

[5]For SDL Studio there seems to be an external app, AnyTM, that allows users to use TMs having different language pairs than the ones in the current translation project. As of Studio 2015, this app has been integrated in the CAT tool and become a new feature. However, this tool does not seem to support the usage of truly multilingual TMs (TMs including several target languages for each segment). For further information on the tool, see: http://www.translationzone.com/openexchange/app/sdltradosstudioanytmtranslationprovider-669.html).

[6]For further information, see: http://kilgray.com/memoq/2015/help-en/index.html?fragment_assembly.html.

for fragments of the source sentence in other TM segments and internally computes their alignment probabilities. It then inserts the translations into the source segment and suggests this new, sometimes partially translated sentence, as a match. Alternatively, only the fragments translated will be inserted in the target segment, one after another, without the source sentence words that could not be retrieved.

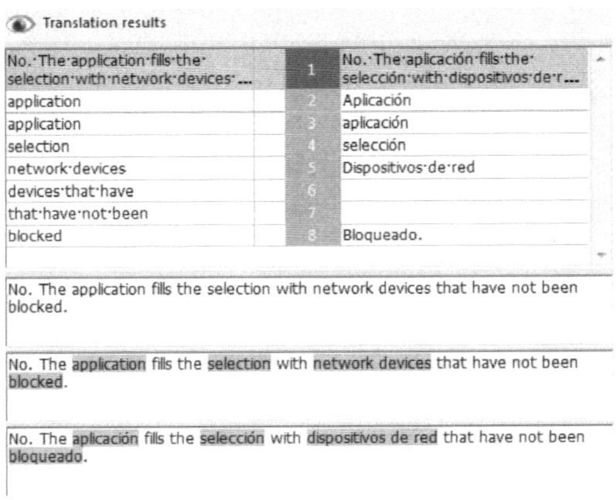

Figure 1: memoQ's fragment assembly functionality.

One limitation of this functionality is that the fragment translations follow the order in which they appear in the source language. Thus, while it may be very useful for pairs of languages which follow a similar structure, it may be problematic for pairs of languages which require reordering. memoQ uses the frequencies of apparition of the fragments to select one translation or another for each particular segment. As a consequence, in some cases the translation selection is wrong, thus yielding wrong translation suggestions.

Examples 1 and 2 show two similar sentences in our TM.

(1) EN: The following message then appears: "Click accept to run the program".
ES: Aparece el siguiente mensaje: "Haga click en aceptar para ejecutar el programa".

(2) EN: The window will show the following: "The application will close".
ES: La ventana mostrará lo siguiente: "Se cerrará la aplicación".

Now imagine we need to translate the sentence in 3.

(3) EN: The following message then appears: "The application will close".

Taking the part of 1 before the colon and the part of 2 after the colon, we would be able to produce the right translation, as shown in 4.

(4) ES: Aparece el siguiente mensaje: "Se cerrará la aplicación".

In technical texts it is often the case that situations like the one just described happen more than once. Thus, it is not surprising that the translators liked the idea and thought it would be nice to find a way of automatically retrieving their translations without having to do concordance searches in the TM. Moreover, remembering that a particular fragment of a segment had been translated in the past is not always possible, as translators may have forgotten it, or different translators may have been involved in the project, thus not seeing fragments of a segment that other translators have translated already.

As this idea seemed to have a great potential to increase the number of TM and fuzzy matches, we decided to implement it and test whether it actually worked. The next Section (4) explains how we proceeded.

4 The new segment generator

As explained in Section 3, we decided to test one idea originated from our internal survey. The idea was to generate new TM segments from fragments of already existing segments. We called our new tool "new segment generator".

The first step was to assess the type of texts that are translated in our company and identify the segment fragments that could be easily extracted. Upon analysis of several sample texts we identified 7 different types of fragments we could work with:

1. Ellipsis
2. Colons
3. Parenthesis
4. Square brackets
5. Curly braces
6. Quotations
7. Text surrounded by tags

In the following subsections (4.1 – 4.3) we describe how each of these types of fragments was treated.

4.1 Ellipsis and colons

One possible type of segment would be that in which an ellipsis ("...") or a colon (":") is used in the middle of the segment. In software localisation or user guides sentences such as the ones in 5 and 6 could appear.

(5) EN: Installing new services... Service XXXX for premium clients: [2]
ES: Instalando nuevos servicios... Servicio XXXX para clientes premium: [2]

(6) EN: You can use the line [abcdef] to describe any of the following characters: a, b, c, d, e, f.
ES: Puede utilizar la línea [abcdef] para describir cualquiera de los siguientes caracteres: a, b, c, d, e, f.

If a different segment only including the text before the ellipsis appears as in Example 7, the TM may not retrieve any fuzzy match. The same would occur with other sentences with colons in which the fragment before or after the colon appears.

(7) Installing new services...

In these cases, we proceeded as follows:

1. Check that there is an ellipsis / a colon on both the source and the target segment.

2. Split the segment in two, being the first part the fragment of the segment up to the ellipsis/colon and the second part the fragment of the segment after the ellipsis/colon.

3. Create a new TM segment for each fragment.

4.2 Parenthesis, square brackets and curly braces

Sometimes, a sentence includes a fragment between parethesis, square brackets or curly braces. The content within such characters may constitute a new segment on its own or appear in a different sentence. At the same time, it may also be the case that the same sentence appears in the text, but without such parenthesis. When sentences like the ones in Examples 8–10 appear, it may thus be desirable to store the translation of the fragment between the aforementioned characters and the sentence without such content.

(8) EN: Creates an installation package for application installation (if it was not created earlier).
ES: Crea un paquete de instalación para la instalación de la aplicación (si no se creó antes).

(9) EN: <return code 1>=[<description>]
ES: <código de retorno 1>=[<descripción>]

(10) EN: Could not open key: [2]. {{ System error [3].}} Verify that you have sufficient access to that key, or contact your support personnel.
ES: Error al abrir la clave: [2]. {{ Error en el sistema [3].}} Compruebe que dispone de los derechos de acceso

The strategy to create new segments was the following:

1. Check that there is content between parenthesis / square brackets / curly braces on both the source and the target segment.

2. Keep three fragments out of each sentence:

   (a) A sentence removing those characters and the content between them.
   (b) A fragment starting at the opening character and finishing on the closing one and including the content within. In this fragment, the parenthesis, square brackets or curly braces are mantained.
   (c) A fragment containing only the content withing those characters (parenthesis, square brackets or curly braces), but without them.

3. Create a new TM segment for each fragment.

At this preliminary stage, we considered that when a sentence has several clauses in parenthesis, square brackets or curly braces, these appear in the same order in the target language. This was done so because for the type of texts used so far to test our application (software manuals) and the pair of languages used (English into Spanish), this seems to be the usual case. In future work, we plan to further evaluate this issue, and consider other ways of ensuring that the right translation is assigned to each clause.

4.3 Quotations and text within tags

Quotations and double tags appearing in the text were handled differently. As the text within the quotations or tags might be part of the sentence where it appears, it could not be removed without adding too much noise to the data. Thus, we identified sentences with quotations and/or tags, we then removed the quotations and/or tags and kept the same sentence without them as a new segment. Finally, we also kept the text within the quotation marks or tags as new segments. Examples 11–12 illustrate this kind of segments.

(11) EN: "You can only set the values of settings that the policy allows to be modified, that is, ""unlocked"" settings."
ES: "Solo se pueden establecer los valores de los parámetros que al directiva permite modificar, es decir, los parámetros ""desbloqueados""."

(12) EN: If you clear the <1>Inherit settings from parent policy</1> check box in the <2>Settings inheritance</2> section of the <3>General</3> section in the properties window of an inherited policy, the ""lock"" is lifted for that policy.
ES: Si anula la selección de la casilla <1>Heredar configuración de la directiva primaria</1> en la sección <2>Herencia de configuración</2> que aparece en la sección <3>General</3> de la ventana de propiedades de una directiva heredada, se abrirá el candado para esa directiva.

5 Pilot test

Before integrating our system in a CAT tool and in our normal production workflows, we deemed it better to run a pilot test. The aim of this test was to measure to which extent the new segments retrieved an increased number of 100% and fuzzy matches.

5.1 Test set

We used as a test set a real translation project coming from one of our clients. It is a software manual written in English and to be translated into Spanish. We selected memoQ 2015 to be the CAT tool used for our testing because it is one of the common CAT tools used by our translators and because we also wanted to measure the impact of our approach when using its "fragment assembly" functionality.

The project had in total 425 segments accounting for 6280 words according to memoQ. Table 1 shows the project statistics as provided by memoQ's analysis tool using the project TM provided by the client. Additionally, memoQ identified 36 segments (418 words) which could be translated benefiting from its "fragment assembly" functionality, which uses fragments of segments to create new translations.

TM match	Words	Segments
Repetitions	1064	80
100%	0	0
95-99%	4	2
85-94%	0	0
75-84%	285	14
50%-74%	2523	187
No Match	2404	142
Total	**6280**	**425**

Table 1: Project statistics according to memoQ using the project TM.

Taking this analysis as the starting point of our pilot test, we generated new segments using the approach described in Section 4. We used three different TMs to further assess whether the size of the translation memory matters for generating translations of segments and retrieving more translations. The first TM (Project TM) was the project TM provided by the client. The second TM (Product TM) was a TM including all projects done for the same product of the client. Finally, the third TM (Client TM) included all projects of that client and thus was the biggest one. Table 2 summarises the size of the three TMs.

	Segments	Words	
		EN	ES
Project TM	16,842	212,472	244,159
		456,631	
Product TM	20,923	274,542	317,797
		592,339	
Client TM	256,099	3,427,861	3,951,732
		7,379,593	

Table 2: Size of the different TMs used.

We then generated new TM segments and stored them as new TMs. Table 3 shows the number of new segments generated using our approach.

Table 4 breaks down the number of segments generated using each strategy and for each TM

	Segments	EN	ES
Project TM new segments	6,776	56,973	66,297
		123,270	
Product TM new segments	7,760	71,034	83,125
		154,159	
new Client TM new segments	74,041	662,714	769,705
		1,432,419	

Table 3: Size of the new TMs generated using our approach.

used. As can be observed, some types are more productive than others. When using the smaller TMs (project and product), the most prolific segment generator category was the one which extracted text surrounded by tags. However, when using the whole client's TM, the text between parenthesis was more prolific.

	TM Proj.	TM Prod.	TM client
Ellipsis	7	6	50
Colon	1801	2094	17894
Parenthesis	1361	1621	**29637**
Square bra.	78	73	598
Curly braces	0	0	0
Quotations	1085	1146	8797
Tags	**2523**	**2892**	17792

Table 4: Number of newly generated segments per type and TM used.

We then tested how many segments would be retrieved using our newly created TMs, both alone and in combination with the TMs we previously had. MemoQ offers the possibility of activating and deactivating different TMs when preparing a file for translation. We thus prepared the project file using 11 combinations to assess which combination performed better as well as whether the new TMs where having any impact in the project. These 11 scenarios were the following:

1. **TM1**: The project TM as provided by the client.
2. **TM2**: Only the new segments generated from the project TM provided by the client.
3. **TM3**: A combination of the project TM and the new segments retrieved from it.
4. **TM4**: Only the new segments generated from the product TM.
5. **TM5**: The project TM and the new segments generated from the product TM.
6. **TM6**: The project TM combined with the new segments TMs generated from the project TM and the ones from the product TM.
7. **TM7**: Only the new segments generated from the client TM.
8. **TM8**: The project TM combined with the new segments generated from the client TM.
9. **TM9**: The project TM combined with the new TMs generated from the client TM and the ones from the project TM.
10. **TM10**: The project TM combined with the new segments generated from the client TM and the ones from the product TM.
11. **TM11**: The project TM combined with the new segments generated from the client TM, the ones from the project TM and the ones from the product TM.

The preparation of a file for translation typically includes both analysing the file and pretranslating it. When the fragment assembly functionality from memoQ is activated, information about how many segments could be translated using fragments is also provided. Tables 5 and 6 summarise the results we obtained for each TM environment when preparing the project for translation.

As can be observed, using the TMs with new segments decreased in all cases the number of segments not started and increased the number of segments translated using fragments (cf. Table 5). It also seems clear that size matters and that the bigger the TM with new fragments, the higher the number of segments that benefit from fragments (cf. TM2, TM4 and TM7 in Table 5).

However, this does not hold true for the pretranslation. In all cases in which the new TMs were used in isolation (TM2, TM4 and TM7) the number of pretranslated segments decreases. This may be due to the fact that those TMs only contain fragments of the original segments present in the different TMs used to generate the segments.

When combined with the project TM, the number of pretranslated segments increases (cf. TM3, TM5, TM6 and TM8-TM11). The best overall results are obtained when using the project TM either in combination with both the new TM generated from the project TM and the new TM gen-

	TM1	TM2	TM3	TM4	TM5	TM6	TM7	TM8	TM9	TM10	TM11
Not started	234	204	150	202	143	143	38	27	**26**	26	**26**
Pre-trans.	155	111	178	108	179	183	139	199	**205**	201	**205**
Fragments	36	110	97	115	103	99	248	199	**194**	198	**194**

Table 5: Overview on the number of segments pre-translated, translated using fragments, or not started.

	TM1	TM2	TM3	TM4	TM5	TM6	TM7	TM8	TM9	TM10	TM11
100%	0	5	5	5	5	5	5	5	**5**	5	**5**
95%-99%	2	3	3	4	4	4	9	9	**9**	9	**9**
85%-94%	0	1	1	1	1	1	2	2	**2**	2	**2**
75%-84%	14	9	14	9	15	15	12	16	**16**	16	**16**
50%-74%	187	130	198	136	202	202	180	223	**226**	226	**226**
No match	142	197	124	190	118	118	137	90	**87**	87	**87**

Table 6: Overview on the number of segments retrieved using the different TMs classified by fuzzy band.

erated from the client's TM (TM9) or combining the three new TMs (TM11). When using the new TM generated from the client TM together with the new product TM (TM10), the number of pretranslated segments decreases slightly (205 → 201), while the number of segments translated using fragments increases slightly (194 → 198).

If we now look at the results obtained in terms of fuzzy matches (cf. Table 6), the same tendencies can be observed. From the very beginning, the number of 100% matches increases from 0 to 5 when using the new TM generated from the project TM. Similarly, the number of matches for the 95–99% fuzzy band also increases (from 2 segments for TM1 up to 9 segments for TM7–TM11), and the 85–94% fuzzy band retrieves a new segment when using the new TM generated from the client TM. The greatest increase in fuzzy matches is experienced by the 50–74% fuzzy band (from 142 segments in TM1 up to 226 in TM9–TM11). Although this band is usually discarded in translation projects as no productivity gains are achieved, an analysis of the new segments retrieved is needed. This would give us potential hints as to what to improve in our new segment generator so that the fuzzy scores are higher. At the same time, it could be the case that our segments are reusable, although the rest of the sentence is not. If this was proven true, a productivity increase may be observed in this band.

In general, it seems that the generation of new TMs using fragments of previously existing segments has a positive effect in the TM fuzzy match retrieval as well as in the generation of translations from fragments that memoQ offers. These positive results indicate that working further on this approach may improve the fuzzy matches and thus enhance the productivity of our translators.

6 Conclusion and future work

In this paper we have explored a new way of generating segments out of previously existing segments. Although we use a naive approach and only make use of punctuation marks and tags to generate such segments, positive results have been obtained in our pilot test. Moreover, as we do not use any type of linguistic information, our approach could be considered language independent.

We are currently working on improving the script that extracts the fragments of segments and generates new ones. This is being done by also analysing in more detail the segments currently retrieved and the segments that could additionally be retrieved. The next step will be to generate yet newer segments by combining the fragments retrieved together and pre-translating files implementing our own "fragment assembly approach" prior to translation. Once this has been done, we will test the final result of our TM population and pre-processing in real projects to measure whether by using this approach translators do translate faster than translating from scratch. This final test will additionally serve as a quality evaluation of the segments newly produced, as we will be able to compare them with the final output produced by translators.

We have also envisioned the combination of already existing methods for retrieving a higher number of TM matches with our system. Among other approaches, it will be interesting to test the inclusion of paraphrasis and semantic similarity methods to create new TM segments (Gupta and Orăsan, 2014; Gupta et al., 2015).

Finally, another potential application of our approach would be the extraction of terminology databases. In many cases, the segments we extract correspond to terms in the source and target text. A closer analysis of them may give us hints about their properties so that we can filter candidate terms and create terminology databases that can be used in combination with the TMs to translate new projects.

Acknowledgments

The research reported in this paper is supported by the People Programme (Marie Curie Actions) of the European Union's Framework Programme (FP7/2007-2013) under REA grant agreement no. 317471.

References

Kevin Flanagan. 2015. Subsegment recall in Translation Memory – perceptions, expectations and reality. *The Journal of Specialised Translation*, (23):64–88, January.

Rohit Gupta and Orăsan. 2014. Incorporating Paraphrasing in Translation Memory Matching and Retrieval. In *Proceedings of the European Association of Machine Translation (EAMT-2014)*.

Rohit Gupta, Constantin Orăsan, Marcos Zampieri, Mihaela Vela, and Josef van Genabith. 2015. Can Translation Memories afford not to use paraphrasing? In *Proceedings of the 18th Annual Conference of the European Association for Machine Translation*, Antalya (Turkey), May. EAMT.

Gábor Hodász and Gábor Pohl. 2005. MetaMorpho TM: a linguistically enriched translation memory. In *Proceedings of the workshop: Modern Approaches in Translation Technologies 2005*, pages 25–30, Borovets, Bulgaria.

Ruslan Mitkov and Gloria Corpas. 2008. Improving Third Generation Translation Memory systems through identification of rehetorical predicates. In *Proceedings of LangTech 2008*.

Viktor Pekar and Ruslan Mitkov. 2007. New Generation Translation Memory: Content-Sensitive Matching. In *Proceedings of the 40th Anniversary Congress of the Swiss Association of Translators, Terminologists and Interpreters*.

Michel Simard and Atsushi Fujita. 2012. A Poor Man's Translation Memory Using Machine Translation Evaluation Metrics. In *Proceedings of the Tenth Conference of the Association for Machine Translation in the Americas*.

Tom Vanallemeersch and Vincent Vandeghinste. 2015. Assessing linguistically aware fuzzy matching in translation memories. In *Proceedings of the 18th Annual Conference of the European Association for Machine Translation*, Antalya (Turkey), May. EAMT.

Spotting false translation segments in translation memories

Eduard Barbu
Translated.net
eduard@translated.net

Abstract

The problem of spotting false translations in the bi-segments of translation memories can be thought of as a classification task. We test the accuracy of various machine learning algorithms to find segments that are not true translations. We show that the Church-Gale scores in two large bi-segment sets extracted from MyMemory can be used for finding positive and negative training examples for the machine learning algorithms. The performance of the winning classification algorithms, though high, is not yet sufficient for automatic cleaning of translations memories.

1 Introduction

MyMemory[1] (Trombetti, 2009) is the biggest translation memory in the world. It contains more than 1 billion bi-segments in approximately 6000 language pairs. MyMemory is built using three methods. The first method is to aggregate the memories contributed by translators. The second method is to use translation memories extracted from corpora, glossaries or data mined from the web. The current distribution of the automatically acquired translation memories is given in figure 1. Approximately 50% of the distribution is occupied by the DGT-TM (Steinberger et al., 2013), a translation memory built for 24 EU languages from aligned parallel corpora. The glossaries are represented by the Unified Medical Language System (UMLS) (Humphreys and Lindberg, 1993), a terminology released by the National Library of Medicine. The third method is to allow anonymous contributors to add source segments and their translations through a web interface.

The quality of the translations using the first method is high and the errors are relatively few.

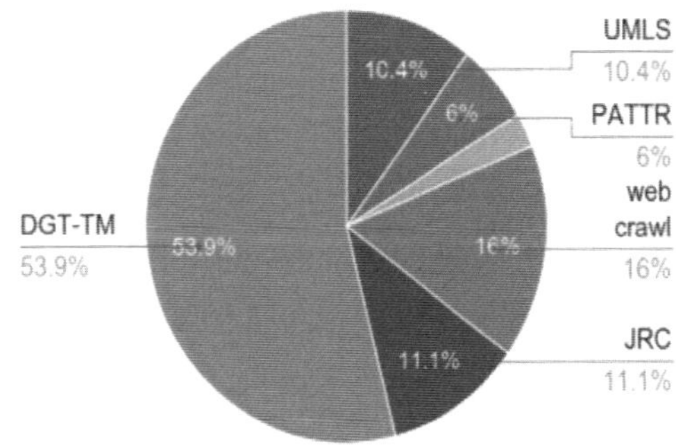

Figure 1: The distribution of automatically acquired memories in MyMemory

However the second method and especially the third one produce a significant number of erroneous translations. The automatically aligned parallel corpora have alignment errors and the collaborative translation memories are spammed or have low quality contributions.

The problem of finding bi-segments that are not true translations can be stated as a typical classification problem. Given a bi-segment a classifier should return yes if the segments are true translations and no otherwise. In this paper we test various classification algorithms at this task.

The rest of the paper has the following structure. Section 2 puts our work in the larger context of research focused on translation memories. Section 3 explains the typical errors that the translation memories which are part of MyMemory contain and show how we have built the training and test sets. Section 4 describes the features chosen to represent the data and briefly describes the classification algorithms employed. Section 5 presents and discusses the results. In the final section we draw the conclusions and plan the further developments.

[1] https://mymemory.translated.net/

Proceedings of the Workshop on Natural Language Processing for Translation Memories (NLP4TM), pages 9–16,
Hissar, Bulgaria, Sept 2015.

2 Related Work

The translation memory systems are extensively used today. The main tasks they help accomplish are localization of digital information and translation (Reinke, 2013). Because translation memories are stored in databases the principal optimization from a technical point of view is the speed of retrieval.

There are two not technical requirements that the translation memories systems should fulfill that interest the research community: the accuracy of retrieval and the translation memory cleaning. If for improving the accuracy of retrieved segments there is a fair amount of work (e.g. (Zhechev and van Genabith, 2010), (Koehn and Senellart, 2010)) to the best of our knowledge the memory cleaning is a neglected research area. To be fair there are software tools that incorporate basic methods of data cleaning. We would like to mention Apsic X-Bench[2]. Apsic X-Bench implements a series of syntactic checks for the segments. It checks for example if the opened tag is closed, if a word is repeated or if a word is misspelled. It also integrates terminological dictionaries and verifies if the terms are translated accurately. The main assumptions behind these validations seem to be that the translation memories bi-segments contain accidental errors (e.g tags not closed) or that the translators sometimes use inaccurate terms that can be spotted with a bilingual terminology. These assumptions hold for translation memories produced by professional translators but not for collaborative memories and memories derived from parallel corpora.

A task somehow similar to translation memory cleaning as envisioned in section 1 is Quality Estimation in Machine Translation. Quality Estimation can also be modeled as a classification task where the goal is to distinguish between accurate and inaccurate translations (Li and Khudanpur, 2009). The difference is that the sentences whose quality should be estimated are produced by Machine Translations systems and not by humans. Therefore the features that help to discriminate between good and bad translations in this approach are different from those in ours.

[2]http://www.xbench.net

3 The data

In this section we describe the process of obtaining the data for training and testing the classifiers. The positive training examples are segments where the source segment is correctly translated by the target segment. The negative training examples are translation memory segments that are not true translations. Before explaining how we collected the examples it is useful to understand what kind of errors the translation memories part of MyMemory contain. They can be roughly classified in the four types :

1. **Random Text**. The Random Text errors are cases when one or both segments is/are a random text. They occur when a malevolent contributor uses the platform to copy and paste random texts from the web.

2. **Chat**. This type of errors verifies when the translation memory contributors exchange messages instead of providing translations. For example the English text "How are you?" translates in Italian as "Come stai?". Instead of providing the translation the contributor answers "Bene" ("Fine").

3. **Language Error**. This kind of errors occurs when the languages of the source or target segments are mistaken. The contributors accidentally interchange the languages of source and target segments. We would like to recover from this error and pass to the classifier the correct source and target segments. There are also cases when a different language code is assigned to the source or target segment. This happens when the parallel corpora contain segments in multiple languages (e.g. the English part of the corpus contains segments in French). The aligner does not check the language code of the aligned segments.

4. **Partial Translations**. This error verifies when the contributors translate only a part of the source segment. For example, the English source segment "Early 1980s. Muirfield C.C." is translated in Italian partially: "Primi anni 1980" ("Early 1980s").

The errors **Random Text** and **Chat** take place in the collaborative strategy of enriching MyMemory. The **Language Error** and **Partial Translations** are pervasive errors.

It is relatively easy to find positive examples because the high majority of bi-segments are correct. Finding good negative examples is not so easy as it requires reading a lot of translation segments. Inspecting small samples of bi-segments corresponding to the three methods, we noticed that the highest percentage of errors come from the collaborative web interface. To verify that this is indeed the case we make use of an insight first time articulated by Church and Gale (Gale and Church, 1993). The idea is that in a parallel corpus the corresponding segments have roughly the same length[3]. To quantify the difference between the length of the source and destination segments we use a modified Church-Gale length difference (Tiedemann, 2011) presented in equation 1 :

$$CG = \frac{l_s - l_d}{\sqrt{3.4(l_s + l_d)}} \quad (1)$$

In figures 2 and 3 we plot the distribution of the relative frequency of Church Gale scores for two sets of bi-segments with source segments in English and target segments in Italian. The first set, from now on called the Matecat Set, is a set of segments extracted from the output of Matecat[4]. The bi-segments of this set are produced by professional translators and have few errors. The other bi-segment set, from now on called the Collaborative Set, is a set of collaborative bi-segments.

If it is true that the sets come from different distributions then the plots should be different. This is indeed the case. The plot for the Matecat Set is a little bit skewed to the right but close to a normal plot. In figure 2 we plot the Church Gale score obtained for the bi-segments of the Matecat set adding a normal curve over the histogram to better visualize the difference from the gaussian curve. For the Matecat set the Church Gale score varies in the interval $-4.18 ... 4.26$.

The plot for the Collaborative Set has the distribution of scores concentrated in the center as can be seen in 3 . In figure 4 we add a normal curve to the the previous histogram. The relative frequency of the scores away from the center is much lower than the scores in the center. Therefore to get a better wiew of the distribution the y axis is reduced to the interval 0...0.1. For the Collaborative set the

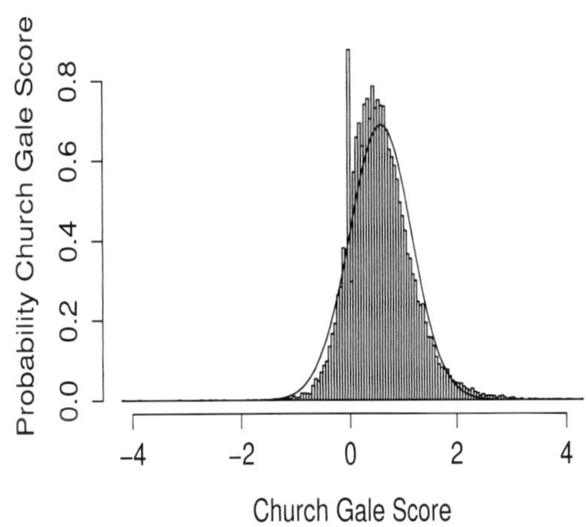

Figure 2: The distribution of Church Gale Scores in the Matecat Set

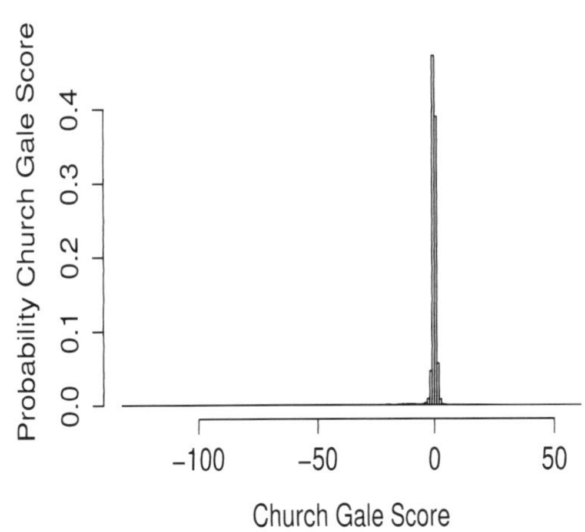

Figure 3: The distribution of Church Gale Scores in the Collaborative Set

[3]This simple idea is implemented in many sentence aligners.

[4]Matecat is a free web based CAT tool that can be used at the following address: https://www.matecat.com

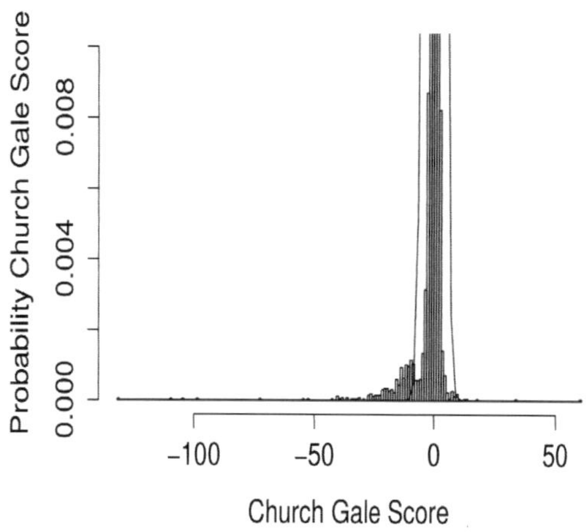

Figure 4: The normal curve added to the distribution of Church Gale Scores in the Collaborative Set

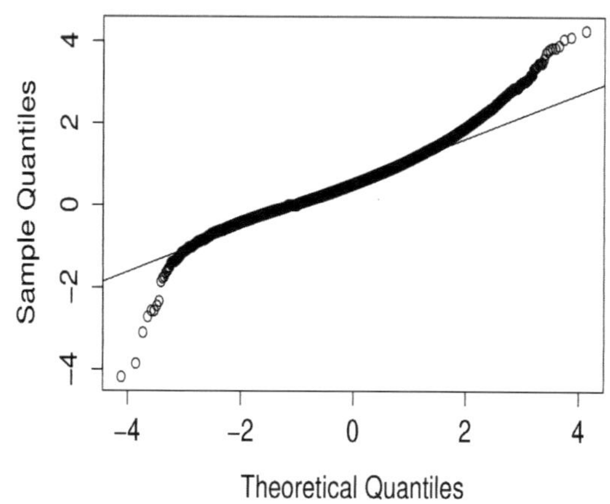

Figure 5: The Q-Q plot for the Matecat set

Church Gale score varies in the interval -131.51 ...60.15.

To see how close the distribution of Church-Gale scores is to a normal distribution we have plotted these distributions against the normal distribution using the Quantile to Quantile plot in figures 5 and 6.

In the Collaborative Set the scores that have a low probability could be a source of errors. To build the training set we first draw random bi-segments from the Matecat Set. As said before the bi-segments in the Matecat Set should contain mainly positive examples. Second, we draw random bi-segments from the Collaborative Set biasing the sampling to the bi-segments that have scores away from the center of the distribution. In this way we hope that we draw enough negative segments. After manually validating the examples we created a training set and a test set distributed as follows :

- **Training Set**. It contains 1243 bi-segments and has 373 negative example.
- **Test Set**. It contains 309 bi-segments and has 87 negatives examples.

The proportion of the negative examples in both sets is approximately 30%.

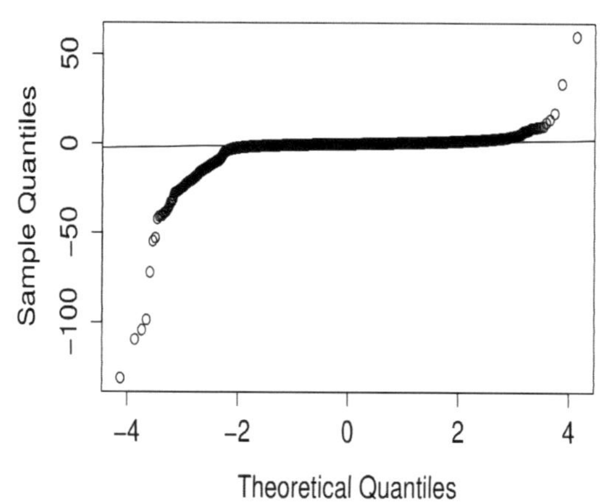

Figure 6: The Q-Q plot for the Collaborative set

4 Machine Learning

In this section we discuss the features computed for the training and the test sets. Moreover, we briefly present the algorithms used for classification and the rationale for using them.

4.1 Features

The features computed for the training and test set are the following :

- *same*. This feature takes two values: 0 and 1. It has value 1 if the source and target segments are equal. There are cases specifically in the collaborative part of MyMemory when the source segment is copied in the target segment. Of course there are perfectly legitimate cases when the source and target segments are the same (e.g. when the source segment is a name entity that has the same form in the target language), but many times the value 1 indicates a spam attempt.

- *cg_score*. This feature is the Church-Gale score described in the equation 1. This score reflects the idea that the length of the source and destination segments that are true translations is correlated. We expect that the classifiers learn the threshold that separates the positive and negative examples. However, relying exclusively on the Church-Gale score is tricky because there are cases when a high Church Gale score is perfectly legitimate. For example, when the acronyms in the source language are expanded in the target language.

- *has_url*. The value of the feature is 1 if the source or target segments contain an URL address, otherwise is 0.

- *has_tag*. The value of the feature is 1 if the source or target segments contain a tag, otherwise is 0.

- *has_email*. The value of the feature is 1 if the source or target segments contain an email address, otherwise is 0.

- *has_number*. The value of the feature is 1 if the source or target segments contain a number, otherwise is 0.

- *has_capital_letters*. The value of the feature is 1 if the source or target segments contain words that have at least a capital letter, otherwise is 0.

- *has_words_capital_letters*. The value of the feature is 1 if the source or target segments contain words that consist completely of capital letters, otherwise is 0. Unlike the previous feature, this one activates only when there exists whole words in capital letters.

- *punctuation_similarity*. The value of this feature is the cosine similarity between the source and destination segments punctuation vectors. The intuition behind this feature is that source and target segments should have similar punctuation vectors if the source segment and the target segment are true translations.

- *tag_similarity*. The value of this feature is the cosine similarity between the source segment and destination segment tag vectors. The reason for introducing this feature is that the source and target segments should contain very similar tag vectors if they are true translations. This feature combines with *has_tag* to exhaust all possibilities (e.g., the tag exists/ does not exist and if it exists is present/is not present in the source and the target segments)

- *email_similarity*. The value of the feature is the cosine similarity between the source segment and destination segment email vectors. The reasoning for introducing this feature is the same as for the feature *tag_similarity*. This feature combines with the feature *has_email* to exhaust all possibilities.

- *url_similarity*. The value of the feature is the cosine similarity between the source segment and destination segment url addresses vectors. The reasoning for introducing this feature is the same as for the feature *tag_similarity*.

- *number_similarity*. The value of the feature is the cosine similarity between the source segment and destination segment number vectors. The reasoning for introducing this feature is the same as for the feature *tag_similarity*.

- *bisegment_similarity*. The value of the feature is the cosine similarity between the destination segment and the source segment translation in the destination language. It formalizes the idea that if the target segment is a true translation of the source segment then a machine translation of the source segment should be similar to the target segment.

- *capital_letters_word_difference*. The value of the feature is the ratio between the difference of the number of words containing at least a capital letter in the source segment and the target segment and the sum of the capital letter words in the bi-segment. It is complementary to the feature *has_capital_letters*.

- *only_capletters_dif*. The value of the feature is the ratio between the difference of the number of words containing only capital letters in the source segment and the target segments and the sum of the only capital letter words in the bi-segment. It is complementary to the feature *has_words_capital_letters*.

- *lang_dif*. The value of the feature is calculated from the language codes declared in the segment and the language codes detected by a language detector. For example, if we expect the source segment language code to be "en" and the target segment language code to be "it" and the language detector detects "en" and "it", then the value of the feature is 0 (en-en,it-it). If instead the language detector detects "en" and "fr" then the value of the feature is 1 (en-en,it-fr) and if it detects "de" and "fr" (en-de,it-fr) then the value is 2.

All feature values are normalized between 0 and 1. The most important features are *bisegment_similarity* and *lang_dif*. The other features are either sparse (e.g. relatively few bi-segments contain URLs, emails or tags) or they do not describe the translation process very accurately. For example, we assumed that the punctuation in the source and target segments should be similar, which is true for many bi-segments. However, there are also many bi-segments where the translation of the source segment in the target language lacks punctuation.

The translation of the source English segment to Italian is performed with the Bing API. The computation of the language codes for the bi-segment is done with the highly accurate language detector Cybozu[5].

4.2 Algorithms

As we showed in section 3 there are cases when the contributors mistake the language codes of the source and target segments. Nevertheless, the segments might be true translations. Therefore, before applying the machine learning algorithms, we first invert the source and target segments if the above situation verifies. We tested the following classification algorithms from the package scikit-learn (Pedregosa et al., 2011):

- **Decision Tree**. The decision trees are one of the oldest classification algorithms. Even if they are known to overfit the training data they have the advantage that the rules inferred are readable by humans. This means that we can tamper with the automatically inferred rules and at least theoretically create a better decision tree.

- **Random Forest**. Random forests are ensemble classifiers that consist of multiple decision trees. The final prediction is the mode of individual tree predictions. The Random Forest has a lower probability to overfit the data than the Decision Trees.

- **Logistic Regression**. The Logistic Regression works particularly well when the features are linearly separable. In addition, the classifier is robust to noise, avoids overfitting and its output can be interpreted as probability scores.

- **Support Vector Machines** with the linear kernel. Support Vector Machines are one of the most used classification algorithms.

- **Gaussian Naive Bayes**. If the conditional independence that the naive Bayes class of algorithm postulates holds, the training converges faster than logistic regression and the algorithm needs less training instances.

- **K-Nearst Neighbors**. This algorithm classifies a new instance based on the distance it has to k training instances. The prediction output is the label that classifies the majority. Because it is a non-parametric method, it can

[5] https://github.com/shuyo/language-detection/blob/wiki/ProjectHome.md

give good results in classification problems where the decision boundary is irregular.

5 Results and discussion

We performed two evaluations of the machine learning algorithms presented in the previous section. The first evaluation is a three-fold stratified classification on the training set. The algorithms are evaluated against two baselines. The first baseline it is called Baseline Uniform and it generates predictions randomly. The second baseline is called Baseline Stratified and generates predictions by respecting the training set class distribution. The results of the first evaluation are given in table 1 :

Algorithm	Precision	Recall	F1
Random Forest	0.95	0.97	0.96
Decision Tree	0.98	0.97	0.97
SVM	0.94	0.98	0.96
K-Nearst Neighbors	0.94	0.98	0.96
Logistic Regression	0.92	0.98	0.95
Gaussian Naive Bayes	0.86	0.96	0.91
Baseline Uniform	0.69	0.53	0.60
Baseline Stratified	0.70	0.73	0.71

Table 1: The results of the three-fold stratified classification.

Excepts for the **Gaussian Naive Bayes** all other algorithms have excellent results. All algorithms beat the baselines by a significant margin (at least 20 points).

The second evaluation is performed against the test set. The baselines are the same as in three-fold evaluation above and the results are in table 2.

The results for the second evaluation are worse than the results for the first evaluation. For example, the difference between the F1-scores of the best performing algorithm: SVM and the stratified baseline is of 10%: twice lower than the difference between the best performing classification algorithm and the same baseline for the first evaluation. This fact might be explained partially by the great variety of the bi-segments in the Matecat and Web Sets. Obviously this variety is not fully captured by the training set.

Algorithm	Precision	Recall	F1
Random Forest	0.85	0.63	0.72
Decision Tree	0.82	0.69	0.75
SVM	0.82	0.81	0.81
K-Nearst Neighbors	0.83	0.66	0.74
Logistic Regression	0.80	0.80	0.80
Gaussian Naive Bayes	0.76	0.61	0.68
Baseline Uniform	0.71	0.72	0.71
Baseline Stratified	0.70	0.51	0.59

Table 2: The results of the classification on the test set.

Unlike in the first evaluation, in the second one we have two clear winners: Support Vector Machines (with the linear kernel) and Logistic Regression. They produce F1-scores around 0.8. The results might seem impressive, but they are insufficient for automatically cleaning MyMemory. To understand why this is the case we inspect the results of the confusion table for the SVM algorithm. From the 309 examples in the test set 175 are true positives, 42 false positives, 32 false negatives and 60 true negatives. This means that around 10% of all examples corresponding to the false negatives will be thrown away. Applying this method to the MyMemory database would result in the elimination of many good bi-segments. We should therefore search for better methods of cleaning where the precision is increased even if the recall drops. We make some suggestions in the next section.

6 Conclusions and further work

In this paper we studied the performance of various classification algorithms for identifying false bi-segments in translation memories. We have shown that the distribution of the Church-Gale scores in two sets of bi-segments that contain different proportion of positive and negative examples is dissimilar. This distribution is closer to the normal distribution for the MateCat set and more sparse for Collective Set. The best performing classification algorithms are Support Vector Machines (with the linear kernel) and Logistic Regression. Both algorithms produce a significant number of false negative examples. In this case the performance of finding the true negative examples does not offset the cost of deleting the false negatives from the database.

There are two potential solutions to this problem. The first solution is to improve the performance of the classifiers. In the future we will study ensemble classifiers that can potentially boost the performance of the classification task. The idea behind the ensemble classifiers is that with differently behaving classifiers one classifier can compensate for the errors of other classifiers. If this solution does not give the expected results we will focus on a subset of bi-segments for which the classification precision is more than 90%. For example, the Logistic Regression classification output can be interpreted as probability. Our hope is that the probabilities scores can be ranked and that higher scores correlate with the confidence that a bi-segment is positive or negative.

Another improvement will be the substitution of the machine translation module with a simpler translation system based on bilingual dictionaries. The machine translation module works well with an average numbers of bi-segments. For example, the machine translation system we employ can handle 40000 bi-segments per day. However, this system is not scalable, it costs too much and it cannot handle the entire MyMemory database. Unlike a machine translation system, a dictionary is relatively easy to build using an aligner. Moreover, a system based on an indexed bilingual dictionary should be much faster than a machine translation system.

Acknowledgments

The research reported in this paper is supported by the People Programme (Marie Curie Actions) of the European Unions Framework Programme (FP7/2007-2013) under REA grant agreement no. 317471.

References

William A. Gale and Kenneth W. Church. 1993. A program for aligning sentences in bilingual corpora. *COMPUTATIONAL LINGUISTICS*.

B. L. Humphreys and D. A. Lindberg. 1993. The UMLS project: making the conceptual connection between users and the information they need. *Bull Med Libr Assoc*, 81(2):170–177, April.

Philipp Koehn and Jean Senellart. 2010. Convergence of translation memory and statistical machine translation. In *Proceedings of AMTA Workshop on MT Research and the Translation Industry*, pages 21–31.

Zhifei Li and Sanjeev Khudanpur. 2009. Large-scale discriminative n-gram language models for statistical machine translation. In *Proceedings of AMTA*.

F. Pedregosa, G. Varoquaux, A. Gramfort, V. Michel, B. Thirion, O. Grisel, M. Blondel, P. Prettenhofer, R. Weiss, V. Dubourg, J. Vanderplas, A. Passos, D. Cournapeau, M. Brucher, M. Perrot, and E. Duchesnay. 2011. Scikit-learn: Machine learning in Python. *Journal of Machine Learning Research*, 12:2825–2830.

Uwe Reinke. 2013. State of the art in translation memory technology. *Translation: Computation, Corpora, Cognition*, 3(1).

Ralf Steinberger, Andreas Eisele, Szymon Klocek, Spyridon Pilos, and Patrick Schlüter. 2013. Dgt-tm: A freely available translation memory in 22 languages. *CoRR*, abs/1309.5226.

Jörg Tiedemann. 2011. *Bitext Alignment*. Number 14 in Synthesis Lectures on Human Language Technologies. Morgan & Claypool, San Rafael, CA, USA.

Marco Trombetti. 2009. Creating the world's largest translation memory.

Ventsislav Zhechev and Josef van Genabith. 2010. Maximising tm performance through sub-tree alignment and smt. In *Proceedings of the Ninth Conference of the Association for Machine Translation in the Americas*.

Improving Translation Memory Matching through Clause Splitting

Katerina Timonera

Research Group in Computational Linguistics

University of Wolverhampton

krtimonera@gmail.com

Ruslan Mitkov

Research Group in Computational Linguistics

University of Wolverhampton

r.mitkov@wlv.ac.uk

Abstract

We propose the integration of clause splitting as a pre-processing step for match retrieval in Translation Memory (TM) systems to increase the number of relevant sub-segment matches. Through a series of experiments, we investigate the impact of clause splitting in instances where the input does not match an entire segment in the TM, but only a clause from a segment. Our results show that there is a statistically significant increase in the number of retrieved matches when both the input segments and the segments in the TM are first processed with a clause splitter.

1 Rationale

Translation memory tools have had a great impact on the translation industry as they provide considerable assistance to translators. They allow translators to easily re-use previous translations, providing them with valuable productivity gains in an industry where there is a great demand for quality translation delivered in the shortest possible time. However, existing tools have some shortcomings. The majority of existing tools rely on Levenshtein distance, and seek to identify matches only at the sentence level. Semantically similar segments are therefore difficult to retrieve if the string similarity is not high enough, as are sub-segment matches because if only part of a sentence matches the input, even if this part is an entire clause, it is unlikely that this sentence would be retrieved (Pekar and Mitkov, 2007). As a result, TMs are especially useful only for highly repetitive text types such as updated versions of technical manuals.

In this study, we aim to address the problem of retrieving sub-segment matches by performing clause splitting on the source segment as a pre-processing step for TM match retrieval. While matches for entire sentences or almost entire sentences are the most useful type of matches, it is also less likely for such matches to be found in most text types, and even less so for complex sentences. Retrieving clauses is desirable because there is a higher chance for a match to be found for a clause than for a complex sentence, and at the same time, clauses are similar to sentences in that they both contain a subject and a verb, hence a "complete thought", therefore clause matches are more likely to be in context and to actually be used by the translator than phrase matches, for example.

We perform experiments comparing the match retrieval performance of TM tools when they are used as is, and when the input file and the TM segments are first processed with a clause splitter before being fed into the TM tool. The paper is organised as follows: In section 2 we discuss related work on TM matching. In section 3 we discuss how clause splitting can be beneficial to TM matching and how clause splitting was implemented for this study. We then describe our experiments in section 4, and discuss the results in section 5. Finally, we present our conclusion and future work in section 6.

Proceedings of the Workshop on Natural Language Processing for Translation Memories (NLP4TM), pages 17–23, Hissar, Bulgaria, Sept 2015.

2 Related Work

Attempts to address the shortcomings of existing tools include the integration of language processing to break down a sentence into smaller segments. The so-called 'second generation' TM system Similis (Planas, 2005) performs chunking to split sentences into syntagmas to allow sub-sentence matching.

However, Reinke (2013) observes that for certain language pairs like English-German, only rather short phrases like simple NPs are identified, and larger syntactic units cannot be retrieved This can be regarded as disadvantage as the processing of larger units would be desirable for the support of professional computer-assisted human translation (Kriele (2006) and Macken (2009), cited in Reinke, 2013).

MetaMorphoTM (Hodász and Pohl, 2005) also divides sentences into smaller chunks. Moreover, it uses a multi-level linguistic similarity technique (surface form, lemma, word class) to determine similarity between two source-language segments.

Other attempts involve deeper linguistic processing techniques. In Pekar and Mitkov (2007) we propose the 'third-generation translation memory' which introduces the concept of semantic matching. We employ syntactic and semantic analysis of segments stored in a TM to produce a generalised representation of segments which reduces equivalent lexical, syntactic and lexico-syntactic constructions into a single representation. Then, a retrieval mechanism operating on these generalised representations is used to search for useful previous translations in the TM.

This study is part of the third-generation translation memory project, of which the ultimate goal is to produce more intelligent TM systems using NLP techniques. To the best of our knowledge, clause splitting has not previously been investigated as a possible method for increasing the number of relevant retrieved matches.

3 Clause splitting for TM matching

Macklovitch and Russel (2000) note that when a sufficiently close match cannot be found for a new input sentence, current TM systems are unable to retrieve sentences that contain the same clauses or other major phrases.

For example, (a) below is a new input sentence composed of twenty five-character words. The TM contains the sentence (b), which shares an identical substring with sentence (a). However, as this substring only makes up only 25% of the sentence's total number of characters, it is unlikely that current TM tools would be able to retrieve it as a fuzzy match.

(a) w1 w2 w3 w4 w5, w6 . . . w20.

(b) w1 w2 w3 w4 w5, w21 . . . w35.

If clause splitting were employed, clauses would be treated as separate segments, thus increasing the likelihood that clauses which are subparts of larger units, could have a match score sufficiently high to be retrieved by the TM system.

In this paper, we compare the effect of performing clause splitting before retrieving matches in a TM. In each experiment, we identify the difference in matching performance when a TM tool is used as is, and when the input file and the translation memory are first run through a clause splitter. The clause splitter we use in this study is a modified version of the one described in Puscasu (2004). The original version employs both machine learning and linguistic rules to identify finite clauses for both English and Romanian, but in this version only the rule-based module is used. Puscasu (2004) developed a clause splitting method for both English and Romanian, and to maintain consistency between the two languages, her definition of a clause is the one prescribed by the Romanian Academy of Grammar, which is that a clause is group of words containing a finite verb. Non/finite and verbless clauses are therefore not considered. The reported F-measure for identifying complete clauses in English is 81.39% (Marsic, 2011).

In this study, the clause splitter is used on both the segments in the input file and the translation memory database. After processing the input and the TM segments with the clause splitter, these were then imported into existing TM tools to examine how well these tools will perform if clause splitting is used in pre-processing.

4 Experiments

Experiments were performed to study the impact of clause splitting when used in pre-processing for the retrieval of segments in a TM. Our hypothesis is that when a clause splitter is used, the number of relevant retrieved matches will increase.

The effect of clause splitting is examined by comparing the number of matches retrieved when TM tools are used as is and when both the input segments and the segments in the translation memory are first processed with a clause splitter before being imported into the TM tools. The tools used are Wordfast Professional 3 and Trados Studio 2009, which are among the most widely used TM tools (Lagoudaki, 2006).

Segments used as the input were selected from the Edinburgh paraphrase corpus (Cohn, Callison-Burch and Lapata, 2008) (in Macken, 2009). We use a paraphrase corpus because we wish to investigate the effect of using a clause splitter in pre-processing to retrieve both segments that contain the entire input clause and segments that do not contain the exact input clause but may still be relevant as they contain a clause that shares a considerable degree of similarity with the input.

We examine the segments retrieved using both the default fuzzy match threshold (75% for Wordfast and 70% for SDL Trados) and the minimum threshold (40% for Wordfast and 30% for Trados). It is not normally recommended for translators to set a low fuzzy match threshold, as this might result in the retrieval of too many irrelevant segments if the translation memory is large. However, in this study, we argue it would be beneficial to examine matches retrieved with the minimum threshold as well. Given that translation memory match scores are mainly calculated using Levenshtein distance, if only one clause in a segment in the TM matches the input, there is a greater chance of the segment being retrieved with a lower threshold. We therefore wish to examine whether the employment of clause splitting will still result in a considerable improvement from using the Levenshtein distance-based matching algorithm in most TM tools if the match threshold setting is already optimised for the retrieval of sub-segment clauses.

It must also be noted that for this study, we are working with the source segments only. Therefore, in the TM files used, both the source and target segments are in English.

We conducted two main sets of experiments referred to as Set A and Set B which are outlined below. In Set A we selected sentences from the Edinburgh corpus that contained more than one clause. We use one clause, or part of it, as the input segment, and we store the entire sentence in the TM. In the experiments where no clause splitting is done, the sentence is stored as is. In the experiments with clause splitting, the original input segments are split into clauses (if there are more than one) and the segments in the TM are the component clauses of the original sentence. For the experiments done without clause splitting, there are 150 input segments and for each one, we test whether the longer corresponding segment in the TM can be retrieved. For the experiments where clause splitting is used, the 150 input segments are split into 180 segments as some of these segments contain more than one clause. We then test whether the corresponding clause from the original longer sentence can be retrieved. An example is presented in Table 1.

The underlined segments are the corresponding segments that should be retrieved.

In Set B there are also 150 input segments for the experiments where no clause splitting is used, and the corresponding segment in the TM is a longer sentence containing a paraphrase of the input segment. For the experiments with clause splitting, there are 185 input segments (as in set A, some of the original 150 have more than one clause) and in the TM, the component clauses of the original longer segment are stored, and we test whether the clause that is a paraphrase of the input can be retrieved. Below is an example.

Without clause splitting	
Input	**Segment in TM**
the ministry of defense once indicated that about 20,000 soldiers were missing in the korean war	the ministry of defense once indicated that about 20,000 soldiers were missing in the korean war and that the ministry of defense believes there may still be some survivors .
With clause splitting	
Input	**Segments in TM**
- the ministry of defense once indicated - that about 20,000 soldiers were missing in the korean war	- the ministry of defense once indicated - that about 20,000 soldiers were missing in the korean war - and that the ministry of defense believes - there may still be some survivors .

Table 1. Set A Example

Without clause splitting	
Input	**Segment in TM**
a member of the chart-topping collective so solid crew dumped a loaded pistol in an alleyway	a member of the rap group so solid crew threw away a loaded gun during a police chase, southwark crown court was told yesterday .
With clause splitting	
Input	**Segments in TM**
a member of the chart-topping collective so solid crew dumped a loaded pistol in an alleyway	- a member of the rap group so solid crew threw away a loaded gun during a police chase , - southwark crown court was told yesterday .

Table 2. Set B Example

5 Results

WORDFAST	W/o clause splitting	W/ clause splitting
% Retrieved (Default threshold)	23.33%	90.00%
% Retrieved (Minimum threshold)	38.00%	92.22%
TRADOS	**W/o clause splitting**	**W/ clause splitting**
% Retrieved (Default threshold)	14.00%	88.89%
% Retrieved (Minimum threshold)	14.00%	96.67%

Table 3. Percentage of correctly retrieved segments in Set A

Table 3 shows the results of the experiments in set A. It is clear that clause splitting considerably increases the number of matches in instances where the input segment can be found in a longer segment stored in the TM. When the corresponding segments that could not be retrieved even with the minimum threshold were analysed, we found that in set A, all instances were due to errors in clause splitting, more specifically the fact that the clause splitter failed to split a sentence containing more than one clause.

Table 4 summarises the percentage of correctly retrieved segments in set B. In this set, it was observed that although the percentage of retrieved matches is generally lower than the percentages in set A, there is still a noticeable increase in the percentage of matches retrieved.

WORDFAST	W/o clause splitting	W/ clause splitting
% Retrieved (Default threshold)	2.67%	17.84%
% Retrieved (Minimum threshold)	10.00%	41.08%
TRADOS	**W/o clause splitting**	**W/ clause splitting**
% Retrieved (Default threshold)	3.33%	25.95%
% Retrieved (Minimum threshold)	36.00%	70.67%

Table 4. Percentage of correctly retrieved segments in Set B

Upon examination of the segments that could not be retrieved even with the default threshold, we found that in both Wordfast and Trados, around 24% had clause splitting errors, such as when a segment is not split at all when it has more than one clause, or when the segment is incorrectly split. As for the rest of the unretrieved segments, we presume that they are so heavily paraphrased that even when clause splitting is performed correctly, the TM tools are still unable to retrieve them.

For each experiment, we conduct a paired t-test using the match scores produced by the TM tools when retrieving each segment (Table 5). When there are no matches or the correct match is not retrieved, the match score is 0. In instances where the original input segment has more than one clause and is thus split by the clause splitter, we take the average match score of the clauses and take this as one case in order to make the results comparable. In all experiments, the difference is significant at the 0.0001 level when computed with SPSS. We can therefore reject the null hypothesis and conclude that there is a statistically significant difference between the results.

SET A			
	Mean		
WORDFAST	Without clause splitting	With clause splitting	p-value
Default threshold	19.23	85.30888891	0.000
Minimum threshold	29.28	86.48888891	0.000
TRADOS	Without clause splitting	With clause splitting	p-value
Default threshold	11.78	83.87777781	0.000
Minimum threshold	11.78	88.07111113	0.000
SET B			
	Mean		
WORDFAST	Without clause splitting	With clause splitting	p-value
Default threshold	2.23	17.21111111	0.000
Minimum threshold	6.49	30.62111112	0.000
TRADOS	Without clause splitting	With clause splitting	p-value
Default threshold	2.71	23.083	0.000
Minimum threshold	16.83	46.36777779	0.000

Table 5. Paired t-test on all experiments

6 Conclusion

Our results show that introducing clause splitting as a pre-processing step in TM match retrieval can significantly increase matching performance in instances where the TM contains segments of which one of the clauses corresponds to the input segment or is a paraphrase of the input segment.

It is worth mentioning that the data used in these experiments are not data imported from the translation memories of practicing translators as they are not easily available. We nevertheless believe that the results of this study provide significant support to the proof-of-concept of third-generation TM systems where NLP processing is expected to improve performance of operational TM systems.

In future work, we wish to incorporate alignment so that on the target side, what is retrieved is not the original target segment but the corresponding clause, as in its current state, our method would only be able to retrieve the original target segment, given that we perform clause splitting only on the source side. It would also be desirable to implement a working TM tool that incorporates clause splitting and examine to what extent these help a translator working on an actual translation project, as the final test of the usefulness of the methods employed is how they actually increase the productivity of translators in terms of time saved.

Acknowledgements

We would like to acknowledge the members of the Research Group in Computational Linguistics at University of Wolverhampton for their support, especially Dr Georgiana Marsic, Dr Constantin Orasan and Dr Sanja Štajner. Part of the research reported in this paper is supported by the People Programme (Marie Curie Actions) of the European Unions Framework Programme (FP7/2007-2013) under REA grant agreement no. 317471.

References

Cohn, T., Callison-Burch, C. and Lapata, M. (2008) Constructing Corpora for the Development and Evaluation of paraphrase systems. *Computational Linguistics*, *34*(4), 597-614.

Hodász, G. and Pohl, G. (2005) MetaMorpho TM: A Linguistically Enriched Translation Memory. In *Proceedings of the International Conference on n Recent Advances in Natural Language Processing (RANLP-05).* Borovets, Bulgaria.

Kriele, C. (2006) Vergleich der Beiden Translation-Memory-Systeme TRADOS und SIMILIS. Diploma thesis. Saarbrücken: Saarland University [unpublished].

Lagoudaki, E. (2006) Translation Memories Survey 2006: Users' Perceptions around TM Use. In *proceedings of the ASLIB International Conference Translating & the Computer* (Vol. 28, No. 1, pp. 1-29).

Macken, L. (2009) In Search of the Recurrent Units of Translation. In *Evaluation of Translation Technology*, ed. by Daelemans, Walter and Véronique Hoste, 195-212. Brussels: Academic and Scientific Publishers.

Macklovitch, E. and Russell, G. (2000) What's been Forgotten in Translation Memory. In *Envisioning machine translation in the information future* (pp. 137-146). Springer Berlin Heidelberg.

Marsic, G. (2011) *Temporal Processing of News: Annotation of Temporal Expressions, Verbal Events and Temporal Relations* [PhD thesis, University of Wolverhampton].

Pekar, V. and Mitkov. R. (2007) New Generation Translation Memory: Content-Sensitive Matching. In *Proceedings of the 40th Anniversary Congress of the Swiss Association of Translators, Terminologists and Interpreters*, 29-30 September 2006, Bern.

Planas, E. (2005) SIMILIS - Second generation TM software. In *Proceedings of the 27th International Conference on Translating and the Computer (TC27).* London, UK.

Puscasu, G. (2004) A Multilingual Method for Clause Splitting. In *Proceedings of the 7th Annual Colloquium for the UK Special Interest Group for Computational Linguistics*.

Reinke, U. (2013) State of the Art in Translation Memory Technology. *Translation: Computation, Corpora, Cognition, 3*(1).

Improving translation memory fuzzy matching by paraphrasing

Konstantinos Chatzitheodorou
School of Italian Language and Literature
Aristotle University of Thessaloniki
University Campus
54124 Thessaloniki, Greece
chatzik@itl.auth.gr

Abstract

Computer-assisted translation (CAT) tools have become the major language technology to support and facilitate the translation process. Those kind of programs store previously translated source texts and their equivalent target texts in a database and retrieve related segments during the translation of new texts. However, most of them are based on string or word edit distance, not allowing retrieving of matches that are similar. In this paper we present an innovative approach to match sentences having different words but the same meaning. We use NooJ to create paraphrases of Support Verb Constructions (SVC) of all source translation units to expand the fuzzy matching capabilities when searching in the translation memory (TM). Our first results for the EN-IT language pair show consistent and significant improvements in matching over state-of-the-art CAT systems, across different text domains.

1 Introduction

The demand of professional translation services has been increased over the last few years and it is forecast to continue to grow for the foreseeable future. Researchers, to support this increasing, have been proposed and implemented new computer-based tools and methodologies that assist the translation process. The idea behind the computer-assisted software is that a translator should benefit as much as possible from reusing translations that have been human translated in the past. The first thoughts can be traced back to the 1960s when the European Coal and Steel Community proposed the development of a memory system that retrieves terms and their equivalent contexts from earlier translations stored in its memory by the sentences whose lexical items are close to the lexical items of the sentence to be translated (Kay, 1980).

Since then, TM systems have become indispensable tools for professional translators who work mostly with content that is highly repetitive such as technical documentation, games and software localization etc. TM systems typically exploit not only exact matches between segments from the document to be translated with segments from previous translations, but also approximate matches (often referred to as fuzzy matches) (Biçici and Dymetman, 2008). As concept, this technique might be more useful for a translator because all the previous human translations become a starting point of the new translation. Furthermore, the whole process is speeded up and the translation quality is more consistent and efficient.

The fuzzy match level refers to all the necessary corrections made by a professional translation in order to make the retrieved suggestion to meet all the standards of the translation process. This effort is typically less than translating the sentence from scratch. To help the translator, CAT tools suggest or highlight all the differences or similarities between the sentences, penaltizing as well the match percent in some cases. However, given the perplexity of a natural language, for similar, but not identical sentences the fuzzy matching level sometimes is too low and therefore the translator is confused.

This paper presents a framework that improves the fuzzy match of similar, but not identical sentences. The idea behind this model is that Y2 which is the translation of Y1 can be the equivalent of X1 given that X1 has the same meaning

Proceedings of the Workshop on Natural Language Processing for Translation Memories (NLP4TM), pages 24–30,
Hissar, Bulgaria, Sept 2015.

with Y1. We use NooJ to create equivalent paraphrases of the source texts to improve as much as possible the translation fuzzy match level given that they share the same meaning but not the same lexical items. In addition to this, we investigate the following questions: (1) is the productivity of the translators improved? (2) are SVC widespread to merit the effort to tackle them? These questions are answered using human centralized evaluations.

The rest of the paper is organized as follows: Section 2 discusses the past related work, section 3 the theoretical background, section 4 the conceptual background as well the architecture of the framework. Section 5 details the experimental results and section 5 the plans for further work.

2 Related work

There has been some work to improve the translation memory matching and retrieval of translation units when working with CAT tools (Koehn and Senellart, 2010; He at al, 2010a; Zhechev and van Genabith, 2010; Wang et al., 2013). Such works aim to improve the machine translation (MT) confidence measures to better predict the human effort in order to obtain a quality estimation that has the potential to replace the fuzzy match score in the TM. In addition to this, these techniques have an effect only in improvement of the MT raw output and not in improvement of fuzzy matching.

A common methodology that gives priority to the human translations is to search first for matches in the project TM. When no such close match is found in the TM, the sentence is machine-translated (He at al, 2010a; 2010b). In a somewhat similar spirit, other hybrid methodologies combine techniques at a sub-sentential level. Most of them, use as much as possible human translations for a given sentence and the unmatched lexical items are machine translated in the target language using a MT system (Smith and Clark, 2009; Koehn and Senellart, 2010; He at al, 2010a; Zhechev and van Genabith, 2010; Wang et al., 2013). Towards the improving of the quality of the MT output, researchers have been using different MT approaches (statistical, rule-based or example-based) trained either on generic or in-domain corpora. Another innovative idea has been proposed by Dong et al. (2014). In their work, they use a lattice representation of possible translations in a monolingual target language corpus to find the potential candidate translations.

On the other hand, various researchers have focused on semantics or syntactic techniques towards improving the fuzzy matching scores in TM but the evaluations they performed were shallow and most of the time limited to subjective evaluation by authors. Thus, this makes it hard to judge how much a semantically informed TM matching system can benefit a professional translator. Planas and Furuse (1999) propose approaches that use lemma and parts of speech along with surface form comparison. In addition to this syntactic annotation, Hodász and Pohl (2005) also include noun phrase (NP) detection (automatic or human) and alignment in the matching process. Pekar and Mitkov (2007) presented an approach based on syntax driven syntactic analysis. Their result is a generalized form after syntactic, lexico-syntactic and lexical generalization.

Another interested approach, similar to ours, has been proposed by Gupta and Orasan (2014). In their work, they generate additional segments based on the paraphrases in a database while matching. Their approach is based on greedy approximation and dynamic programming given that a particular phrase can be paraphrased in several ways and there can be several possible phrases in a segment which can be paraphrased. It is an innovative technique, however, paraphrasing lexical or phrasal units in not always safe and in some cases, it can confuse rather than help the translator. In addition to this, a paraphrase database is required for each language.

Even if the experimental results show significant improvements in terms of quality and productivity, the hypotheses are produced by a machine using unsupervised methods and therefore the post-editing effort might be higher comparing to human translation hypotheses. To the best of our knowledge, there is no similar work in literature because our approach does not use any MT techniques given that target side of the TM remains "as is". To improve the fuzzy matching, we paraphrase the source translation units of the TM, so that a higher fuzzy match will be identified for sentences sharing the same meaning. Therefore, the professional translator is given a human translated segment that is the paraphrase of the sentence to be translated. This ensures that no out-of-domain lexical items or no machine translation errors will appear in the hypotheses, making the post-editing process trivial.

3 Theoretical background

There are several implementations of the fuzzy match estimation during the translation process, and commercial products typically do not disclose the exact algorithm they use (Koehn, 2010). However, most of them are based on the word and/or character edit distance (Levenshtein distance) (Levenshtein, 1966) i.e., the total number of deletions, insertions, and substitutions in order the two sentences become identical (Hirschberg, 1997).

For instance, the word-based string edit distance between sentence (1) and (2) is 70% (1 substitution and 3 deletions for 13 words), and the character-based string edit distance is 76% (14 deletions for 60 characters) without counting whitespaces based on Koehn's (2010) formula for fuzzy matching. This is a low score and many translators may decide not to use it and therefore not to gain from it.

(1) Press ' Cancel ' to **make the cancellation** of your personal information .

(2) Press ' Cancel ' to **cancel** your personal information .
(3) Premere ' Cancel ' per cancellare i propri dati personali .

(4) Press ' Cancel ' to **cancel** your booking information .

In this case, according to methodologies proposed by researchers of this field, this sentence will be sent for machine translation given the low fuzzy match score and then it should be post-edited. Otherwise, the translator should translate it from scratch. However, this is not always safe, given that in many cases post-editing MT output requires more time than translating from scratch.

Observing the differences between sentences (1) and (2) one can easily conclude that they share the same meaning although they don't share the same lexical items. This happens because of their syntax. In more detail, sentence (1) contains a SVC while sentence (2) contains its nominalization. An EN-IT professional translator can benefit from our approach by accepting the sentence (3) as the equivalent translation of the sentence (1).

SVCs, like *make a cancellation*, are verb-noun complexes which occur in many languages. Form a syntactic and semantic point of view they act in the same way as multi-word units. Their meaning is mainly reflected by the predicate noun, while the support verb is often semantically reduced. The support verb contributes little content to its sentence; the main meaning resides with the predicate noun (Barreiro, 2008).

SVCs include common verbs like *give*, *have*, *make*, *take*, etc. Those types of complexes can be paraphrased with a full verb, maintaining the same meaning. While support verbs are similar to auxiliary verbs regarding their meaning contribution to the clauses in which they appear, support verbs fail the diagnostics that identify auxiliary verbs and are therefore distinct from auxiliaries (Butt, 2003).

SVCs challenge theories of compositionality because the lexical items that form such constructions do not together qualify as constituents, although the word combinations do qualify as catenae. The distinction of a SVC from other complex predicates or arbitrary verb-noun combinations is not an easy task, especially because their syntax that is not always fixed. Except of some cases, they appear with direct object (e.g. *to make attention*) or with direct object (e.g. *to make a reservation*) (Athayde, 2001).

Our approach paraphrases SVCs found in the source translation units of a TM in order to increase the fuzzy matching between sentences having the same meaning. It is a safe technique because the whole process has no effect on the target side of the TM translation units. Hence, the translators benefit only from human translation hypotheses that usually are linguistically correct.

In our example, an EN-IT translator will receive an exact match during his performance when translating the sentence (1) given the English sentence (2) and its Italian equivalent (sentence (3)) that is included in the TM. In addition to this, in case of translating the sentence (4), the fuzzy match score would be around 90% (1 substitution for 10 words) comparing to 61% with no-paraphrase (2 substitution and 3 deletions for 13 words). Other than fuzzy match, according to Barreiro (2008) machine-translation of SVCs is hard, so the expected output from the machine will not be good enough. In our example, "cancel" can be either a verb or noun.

4 Conceptual background

As already discussed, paraphrasing a SVC can increase the fuzzy match level during the translation process. This section details the pipeline of modules towards the paraphrase of the TM source translation units.

4.1 NooJ

The main component of our framework is NooJ (Silberztein, 2003). NooJ is a linguistic development environment used to construct large-coverage formalized descriptions of natural languages, and apply them to large corpora, in real time. The module consists of a very large lexicon, along with a large set of local grammars to recognize named entities as well as unknown words, word sequences etc. These resources have been obtained from OpenLogos, an old open source rule-based MT system (Scott and Barreiro, 2009). In NooJ, an electronic dictionary contains the lemmas with a set of information such as the category/part-of-speech (e.g. V for verbs, A for adjectives etc.), one or more inflectional and/or derivational paradigms (e.g. how to conjugate verbs, how to lemmatize or nominalize them etc.), one or more syntactic properties (e.g. +transitiv for transitive verbs or +PREPin etc.), one or more semantic properties (e.g. distributional classes such as +Human, domain classes such as +Politics) and finally, one or more equivalent translations (+IT="translation equivalent"). Figure 1 illustrates typical dictionary entries.

artist,N+FLX=TABLE+Hum
cousin,N+FLX=TABLE+Hum
pen,N+FLX=TABLE+Conc
table,N+FLX=TABLE+Conc
man,N+FLX=MAN+Hum

Figure 1: Dictionary entries in NooJ for nouns.

4.2 Paraphrasing the source translation units

The generation of the TM that contains the paraphrased translation units is straightforward. The architecture of the process which is summarized in Figure 2, is performed in three pipelines:

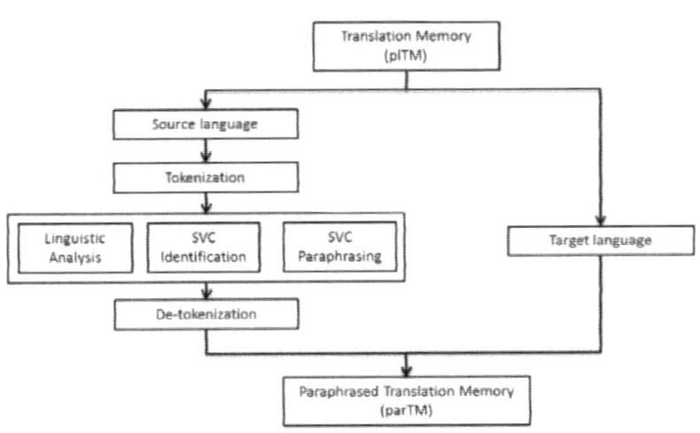

Figure 2: Pipeline of the paraphrase framework.

The first pipeline includes the extraction of the source translation units of a given TM. The target translation units are protected so that they will not be parsed by the framework. This step also includes the tokenization process. Tokenization of the English data is done using Berkeley Tokenizer (Petrov et al., 2006). The same tool is also used for the de-tokenization process in the last step.

Then, all the source translation units pass through NooJ to identify the SVCs using the local grammar of Figure 3. To do so, NooJ first pre-processes and analyses the text based on specific dictionaries and grammars attached in the module. This is a crucial step because if the text is not correctly analyzed, the local grammar will not identify all the potential SVCs and therefore there will not be any gain in terms of fuzzy matching. Once the text is analyzed, all the possible SVCs are identified and hence paraphrased.

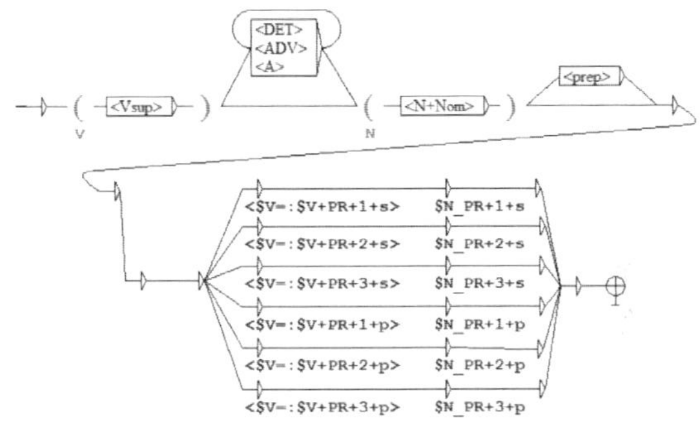

Figure 3: Local grammar for identification and paraphrasing of SVCs.

In more detail, the local grammar checks for a support verb followed by a determiner, adjective or adverb (optionally), a nominalization and optionally by a preposition, and generates the verbal paraphrases in the same tense and person as the source. We should notice that this graph recognizes and paraphrases only SVCs in simple present indicative tense. However, our NooJ module contains grammars created for the all the other grammatical tenses and moods that follow the same structure. The elements in red colors characterize the variables as verb and predicate nouns. The elements **<$V=:$V+PR+1+s>**, and **$N_PR+1+s** represent lexical constraints that are displayed in the output, such as specification of the support verb that belongs to a specific SVC. These particular elements refer to the first person singular of the simple present tense. The predicate noun is identified, mapped to its deriver and displayed as a full verb while the other elements of the sentence are eliminated. The final output of NooJ is a sentence that contains the paraphrase instead of the SVCs, were applicable.

The last pipeline contains the de-tokenization as well as the concatenation of the paraphrased translation units in the original TM, if any. The paraphrased translation units have the same proprietaries, tags etc., as the original units.

This TM should be imported and used in the same way as before in all CAT tools. As of now, our approach can be applied only to TMs that have the English language as source. As mentioned earlier, there is no limit for the target language given that we apply our approach only to the source language translation units.

5 Experimental results

The aim of this research is to provide translators with fuzzy match scores higher than before in case the TM contains a translation unit which has the same meaning with the sentence to be translated. Given that there is no automatic evaluation for this purpose, we formulate this as a ranking problem. In this work, we analyze a set of 100 sentences from automotive domain and 100 from IT domain to measure the difference of the fuzzy match scores between our approach (parTM) and the conversional translation process, where a plain TM is used (plTM). This test set, was selected manually in order to contain SVCs in order to ensure that each sentence contains at least one SVC.

Our method has been applied to a TM which contained 1025 EN-IT translation units. Our module recognized 587 SVCs, so the generated TM (parTM) was contained 1612 translation units (1025 original + 587 paraphrases). The TM contains translations that have been taken from a larger TM based on the degree of fuzzy match that at least meets the minimum threshold of 50%. To create the analysis report logs we used Trados Studio 2014[1].

The results of both analyses are given in Table 1.

Our paraphrased TM attains state-of-the-art performance on increasing the fuzzy match leveraging. It is interesting to note that the highest gains are achieved in the low fuzzy categories (0%-74%). However, we achieve extremely high numbers in other categories. Our approach improves the scores by 17% in 100% match category, 5% in category 95% - 99%, 6% in category 85% - 94%, 28% in category 75% - 84% and finally, 27% in category 0%-74% (No match + 50%-74%). This is a clear indication that paraphrasing of SVCs significantly improves the retrieval results and hence the productivity.

Fuzzy match category	**plTM**	**parTM**
100%	14	48
95% - 99%	23	32
85% - 94%	18	29
75% - 84%	51	38
50% - 74%	32	18
No Match	62	35
Total	**200**	**200**

Table 1: Statistics for experimental data

To check the quality of the retrieved segments human judgment was carried by professional translators. The test set consist of retrieved segments with fuzzy match score >=85% (108 segments). The motivation for this evaluation is twofold. Firstly to show how much impact paraphrasing of SVCs has in terms of retrieval and secondly to see the translation quality of those segments which the fuzzy match score is improved because of the paraphrasing process.

According to translators, paraphrasing helps and speeds up the translation process. Moreover, the fact that the target segments remain "as is" encourage them to use it without a second thought.

Figure 4 shows two cases where translators selected to use segments from the parTM. We can see that paraphrasing not only helps to increase the retrieving but also ensures that the proposed translation is a human translation, so no errors will appear and less post editing is required in case of not equal to 100%.

While there are some drops in terms of fuzzy match improvement, our system presents few weaknesses. Most of them regard the out-of-vocabulary words during the analysis process by NooJ. Although our NooJ module contains a very large lexicon, along with a very large set of local grammars to recognize and paraphrase SVCs, a few translation units (6 segments) were not paraphrased. In addition to this, 2 segments were paraphrased incorrectly. This happens because they contain either out-of-vocabulary words or due to their syntax complexity. This is one of our approach's weaknesses that will be addressed for future projects.

Seg:	**Make sure** that the brake hose is not twisted.
TMsl: TMtg	**Ensure** that the brake hose is not twisted **Assicurarsi** che il tubo flessibile freni non sia attorcigliato.

[1] http://www.sdl.com/cxc/language/translation-productivity/trados-studio/

parTMsl:	**Make sure** that the brake hose is not twisted.

Seg:	CAUTION: You must **make the istallation** of the version 6 of the software.
TMsl:	CAUTION: You **must install** the version 6 of the software.
TMtg	ATTENZIONE: Si **deve installare** la versione 6 del software.
parTMsl	CAUTION: You must **make the istallation** of the version 6 of the software.

Figure 4: Accepted translations.

6 Conclusion

In this paper, we have presented a method that improves the fuzzy match of similar, but not identical sentences. We use NooJ to create equivalent paraphrases of the source texts to improve as much as possible the translation fuzzy match level given that the meaning is the same but they don't share the same lexical items.

The hybridization strategy implemented has already been evaluated with different experiments, translators, text types and language pairs, which showed that it is very effective. The results show that for all fuzzy-match ranges our approach performs markedly better than the plain TM for different fuzzy match levels, especially for low fuzzy match categories. In addition to this, the translators' satisfaction and trust is abundant comparing to MT approaches.

In the future, we will continue to explore ways paraphrasing of other support verbs and other support languages as well. Last but not least, a paraphrase framework to the target sentence may improve even more the quality of translations.

References

Athayde M. F. 2001. *Construções com verbo-suporte (funktionsverbgefüge) do português e do alemão*. In Cadernos do CIEG Centro Interuniver-sitário de Estudos Germanísticos. n. 1. Coimbra, Portugal: Universidade de Coimbra

Barreiro A. 2008. *Make it simple with paraphrases: Automated paraphrasing for authoring aids and machine translation*. Ph. D. thesis, Universidate do Porto

Biçici E and Dymetman M 2008. *Dynamic Translation Memory: Using Statistical Machine Translation to improve Translation Memory Fuzzy Matches*. In Proceedings of the 9th International Conference on Intelligent Text Processing and Computational Linguistics (CICLing 2008), LNCS, Haifa, Israel, February 2008.

But M. 2003. *The Light Verb Jungle*. In Harvard Working Papers in Linguistics, ed. G. Aygen, C. Bowern, and C. Quinn. 1–49. Volume 9, Papers from the GSAS/Dudley House workshop on light verbs.

Dong M., Cheng Y., Liu Y., Xu J., Sun M., Izuha T., and Hao J. 2014. *Query lattice for translation retrieval*. In COLING.

Gupta R. and Orasan C. 2014. *Incorporating Paraphrasing in Translation Memory Matching and Retrieval*. In Proceedings of the 17th Annual Conference of European Association for Machine Translation.

He Y., Ma Y., van Genabith J., and Way A. 2010a. *Bridging SMT and TM with translation recommendation*. In ACL.

He Y., Ma Y., Way A., and Van Genabith J. 2010b. *Integrating n-best SMT outputs into a TM system*. In COLING.

Hirschberg Daniel S. 1997. *Serial computations of Levenshtein distances*. Pattern matching algorithms, Oxford University Press, Oxford.

Hodász G., & Pohl G. 2005. *MetaMorpho TM: a linguistically enriched translation memory*. In In international workshop, modern approaches in translation technologies.

Kay M. 1980. *The proper place of men and machines in language translation*. Palo Alto, CA: Xerox Palo Alto Research Center, October 1980; 21pp.

Koehn P. and Senellart J. 2010. *Convergence of translation memory and statistical machine translation*. In AMTA.

Levenshtein Vladimir I. 1966. *Binary codes capable of correcting deletions, insertions, and reversals*. In Soviet physics doklady, volume 10, pages 707–710.

Pekar V., & Mitkov R. 2007. *New Generation Translation Memory: Content-Sensivite Matching*. In Proceedings of the 40th anniversary congress of the swiss association of translators, terminologists and interpreters.

Petrov S., Leon B., Romain T, and Dan K. 2006. *Learning accurate, compact, and interpretable tree annotation*. In Proceedings of the COLING/ ACL, pages 433–440.

Planas E., & Furuse O. 1999. *Formalizing Translation Memories*. In Proceedings of the 7th machine translation summit (pp. 331–339).

Scott B, Barreiro A 2009. *Openlogos MT and the SAL representation language*. In: Proceedings of the first international workshop on free/open-source rule-based machine translation, Alacant, pp 19–26

Silberztein M. 2003. *NooJ manual*. Available at http://www.nooj4nlp.net

Smith J. and Clark S. 2009. *Ebmt for SMT*: A new EBMT-SMT hybrid. In EBMT.

Wang K., Zong C., and Su K.-Y. 2014. *Dynamically integrating cross-domain translation memory into phrase-based machine translation during decoding*. In COLING.

Zhechev V. and van Genabith J. 2010. *Seeding statistical machine translation with translation memory output through tree-based structural alignment*. In SSST.

Increasing Coverage of Translation Memories with Linguistically Motivated Segment Combination Methods

Vít Baisa, Aleš Horák, Marek Medveď
Natural Language Processing Centre, Masaryk University, Brno, Czech Republic
{xbaisa,hales,xmedved1}@fi.muni.cz

Abstract

Translation memories (TMs) used in computer-aided translation (CAT) systems are the highest-quality source of parallel texts since they consist of segment translation pairs approved by professional human translators. The obvious problem is their size and coverage of new document segments when compared with other parallel data.

In this paper, we describe several methods for expanding translation memories using linguistically motivated segment combining approaches concentrated on preserving the high translational quality. The evaluation of the methods was done on a medium-size real-world translation memory and documents provided by a Czech translation company as well as on a large publicly available DGT translation memory published by European Commission. The asset of the TM expansion methods were evaluated by the pre-translation analysis of widely used MemoQ CAT system and the METEOR metric was used for measuring the quality of fully expanded new translation segments.

1 Introduction

Most professional translators use a specific CAT system with provided or self-built translation memories (TM). The translation memories are usually in-house, costly and manually created resources of varying sizes of thousands to millions of translation pairs.

Only recently some TMs have been made publicly available: DGT (Steinberger et al., 2013), or MyMemory (Trombetti, 2009); to mention just a few. But there is still a heavy demand on enlarging and improving TMs and their coverage of new input documents to be translated.

Obviously, the aim is to have a TM that best fits to the content of a new document as this is crucial for speeding up the translation process: when a larger part of a document can be pre-translated by a CAT system, the translation itself can be cheaper. Coverage of TMs is directly translatable to savings by translation companies and their customers.

We present two methods for expanding TMs: subsegment generation and subsegment combination. The idea behind these methods is based on the fact, that even if the topic of the new document is well covered by the memory, only very rarely the memory includes exact sentences (segments) as they appear in the document. The differences between known and new segments often consist of substitutions or combinations of particular known subsegments.

The presented methods concentrate on increasing the coverage of the content of an existing TM with regard to a new document, and at the same time try to keep a reasonable quality of newly generated segment pairs. We work with English-Czech data but the procedures are mostly language independent.

Evaluation was done on several documents and a medium-size in-house translation memory provided by a large Czech translation company. For comparison, we have also tested the methods on the DGT translation memory.

2 Related work

Translation memories are generally understudied within the field of NLP. Machine translation techniques, especially *example-based machine translation* (*EBMT*) employ translation memories in an approach similar to CAT systems (Planas and Furuse, 1999) but NLP approaches have not been applied on them extensively.

TM-related papers mainly focus on algorithms for searching, matching and suggesting segments

Proceedings of the Workshop on Natural Language Processing for Translation Memories (NLP4TM), pages 31–35,
Hissar, Bulgaria, Sept 2015.

CZ	EN	probabilities				alignment	
být větší	be greater	0.538	0.053	0.538	0.136	0-0	1-1
být větší	be larger	0.170	0.054	0.019	0.148	0-0	1-1

Figure 1: An example of generated subsegments – consistent phrases

within CAT systems (Planas and Furuse, 2000).

In (Désilets et al., 2008), the authors have attempted to build translation memories from Web since they found that human translators in Canada use Google search results even more often than specialized translation memories. That is why they developed system *WeBiText* for extracting possible segments and their translations from bilingual web pages.

In the study (Nevado et al., 2004), the authors exploited two methods of segmentation of translation memories. Their approach starts with a similar assumption as our subsegment combination methods presented below, i.e. that a TM coverage can be increased by splitting the TM segments to smaller parts (subsegments). In both cases, the subsegments are generated via the phrase-based machine translation (PBMT) technique (Koehn et al., 2003). However, our methods do not present the subsegments as the results. The subsegments are used in segment combination methods to obtain new larger translational phrases, or full segments in the best case.

(Simard and Langlais, 2001) describes a method of sub-segmenting translation memories which deals with the principles of EBMT. The authors of this study created an on-line system TransSearch (Macklovitch et al., 2000) for searching possible translation candidates within all subsegments in already translated texts. These subsegments are linguistically motivated—they use a text-chunker to extract phrases from the Hansard corpus.

3 Subsegment generation

In the first step, the proposed TM expansion methods process the available translation memory and generate all *consistent phrases* as subsegments from it. Subsegments and the corresponding translations are generated using the Moses (Koehn et al., 2007) tool directly from the TM, no additional data is used.

The word alignment is based on MGIZA++ (Gao and Vogel, 2008) (parallel version of GIZA++ (Och and Ney, 2003)) and the default Moses heuristic *grow-diag-final*.[1] The next steps are phrase extraction and scoring (Koehn et al., 2007). The corresponding extended TM is denoted as SUB. The output from subsegment generation contains for each subsegment its translation, probabilities and alignment points, see Figure 1 for an example.

The four probabilities are *inverse phrase translation probability*, *inverse lexical weighting*, *direct phrase translation probability* and *direct lexical weighting*, respectively. They are obtained directly from Moses procedures. These probabilities are used to select the best translations in case there are multiple translations for a subsegment. Alternative translations for a subsegment are combined from different aligned pairs in the TM. Typically, short subsegments have many translations.

The alignment points determine the word alignment between subsegment and its translation, i.e. *0-0 1-1* means that the first word *být* from source language is translated to the first word in the translation *be* and the second word *větší* to the second *greater*. These points give us important information about the translation: 1) empty alignment, 2) one-to-many alignment and 3) opposite orientation.

4 Subsegment combination

The output of the subsegment generation is denoted as a special translation memory named SUB. The obtained subsegments are then filtered and used by the following methods for subsegment combination with regard to the segments from the input document:

- JOIN: new segments are built by concatenating two segments from SUB, output is J.
    1. JOIN:O: joint subsegments overlap in a segment from the document, output=OJ.
    2. JOIN:N: joint subsegments neighbour in a segment from the document, output=NJ.

[1] http://www.statmt.org/moses/?n=FactoredTraining.AlignWords

Table 1: An example of the SUBSTITUTE:O method, Czech → English.

original subsegments	• "lze rozdělit do těchto kategorií:" (*can be divided into these categories:*) • "následujících kategorií" (*the following categories*)
new subsegment	"lze rozdělit do následujících kategorií:"
its translation	*can be divided into the following categories:*

- SUBSTITUTE: new segments can be created by replacing a part of one segment with another subsegment from SUB, output is S.

  1. SUBSTITUTE:O: the gap in the first segment is covered with an overlap with the second subsegment, see the example in Table 1, output is OS.
  2. SUBSTITUTE:N: the second subsegment is inserted into the gap in the first segment, output is NS.

During the subsegment non-overlapping combination, the acceptability of the combination is decided (and ordered) by measuring a language fluency score obtained by a combined n-gram score (for $n = \langle 1..5 \rangle$) from a target language model.[2] The quality of the subsegment translation can be increased by filtering the used subsegments on noun phrase boundaries.

The algorithm for the JOIN method actually works with indexes which represent the subsegment positions in the tokenized segment. The available subsegments are processed as a list I ordered by the subsegment size (in the number of tokens, in descending order). The process starts with the biggest subsegment in the segment and then tries to join it successively with other subsegments. If it succeeds, the new subsegment is appended to a temporary list T. After all other subsegments are processed, the temporary list T of new subsegments is prepended to I and the algorithm starts with a new subsegment created from the two longest subsegments. If it does not succeed, the next subsegment in the order is processed. The algorithm thus prefers to join longer subsegments. In each iteration it generates new (longer) subsegments and it discards one processed subsegment.

[2]In current experiments, we have trained a language model using KenLM (Heafield, 2011) tool on first 50 million sentences from the enTenTen corpus (Jakubíček et al., 2013).

5 Evaluation

For the evaluation of the proposed methods, we have used a medium-size in-house translation memory provided by a Czech translation company and two real-world documents of nearly 5,000 segments with their referential translations. The TM contains 144,311 Czech-English translation pairs filtered from the complete company's TM by the same topic as the tested documents. For a comparison, we have run and evaluated the methods also on publicly available DGT translation memory (Steinberger et al., 2013) with the size over 300,000 translation pairs.

For measuring coverage of the expanded TMs we have used the document and TM analysis tool included in the MemoQ software. The same evaluation is used by translation companies for an assessment of the actual translation costs. The results have been obtained directly from the pre-translation analysis of the MemoQ system. The results are presented in Table 2. The TM column contains the results for the original non-expanded translation memory. The column SUB displays the analysis for subsegments (consistent phrases) derived from the original TM. The other columns correspond to the methods JOIN, see Section 4. The final column "all" is the resulting expanded TM obtained as a combination of all tested methods. All numbers represent coverage of segments from the input document versus segments from expanded TMs. The analysis divides all matches segments to categories (lines in the tables. Each category denotes how many words from the segment were found in the analysed TM. 100% match corresponds to the situation when a whole segment from D can be translated using a segment from the respective TM. Translations of shorter parts of the segment are then matches lower than 100%. The most valuable matches for translation companies and translators are those over 75–85%. The presented results show an analysis of the expanded TM for documents with 4,563 segments (35,142 words and 211,407 characters).

Table 2: MemoQ analysis, TM, coverage in %.

Match	TM	SUB	OJ	NJ	all
100%	0.41	0.12	0.10	0.17	**0.46**
95–99%	0.84	0.91	0.64	0.90	1.37
85–94%	0.07	0.05	0.25	0.76	0.81
75–84%	0.80	0.91	1.71	3.78	4.40
50–74%	8.16	10.05	25.09	40.95	42.58
any	10.28	12.04	27.79	46.56	**49.62**

Table 3: MemoQ analysis, DGT-TM.

Match	SUB	OJ	NJ	all
100%	0.08	0.07	0.11	**0.28**
95–99%	0.75	0.44	0.49	0.66
85–94%	0.05	0.08	0.49	0.61
75–84%	0.46	0.96	3.67	3.85
50–74%	10.24	27.77	41.90	44.47
all	11.58	29.32	46.66	**49.87**

For a comparison we also tested the methods on DGT translation memory (Steinberger et al., 2013). We have used 330,626 pairs from 2014 release. See Table 3 for the results of DGT alone and Table 4 for combination of the TM and DGT.

Table 4: MemoQ analysis, TM + DGT-TM.

Match	SUB	OJ	NJ	all
100%	0.15	0.13	0.29	**0.57**
95–99%	0.98	0.59	1.24	1.45
85–94%	0.09	0.22	1.34	1.37
75–84%	1.03	2.26	6.35	7.07
50–74%	12.15	34.84	49.82	51.62
all	14.40	38.04	59.04	**61.51**

We have also compared the results with the output of a function called *Fragment assembly* (Teixeira, 2014), that is present in the MemoQ CAT system.[3] Fragment assembly suggests new segments based on several dictionary and non-word elements (term base, non-translatable hits, numbers, auto-translatable hits). Unknown subsegments are taken from the source language in the tested setup. For measuring the quality of translation (accuracy), we have used METEOR metric (Denkowski and Lavie, 2014). We have achieved score 0.29 with our data in comparison with MemoQ CAT system with score 0.03 when computed for all segments including those with empty translations to the target language. When we take into account just the segments that are pre-translated by MemoQ Fragment assembly as well as by our methods (871 segments), we have achieved the score of 0.36 compared to 0.27 of MemoQ. As the METEOR evaluation metric has been proposed to evaluate MT systems, it assumes that we have fully translated segments (pairs). We have thus provided a "mixed" translation in the same way as it is done in the MemoQ Fragment assembly technique – non-translated phrases (subsegments) appear in the output segment "as is", i.e. in the source language. The resulting segment can thus be a combination of source and target language words, which is correspondingly taken into account by the METEOR metric. We have also measured the asset of particular methods with regard to the translation quality, however, in this case we have measured just full 100% matched segments. The results are presented in Table 5. Nevertheless this evaluation was done for the sake of completeness. It is well known that automatic evaluation metrics for assessing machine translation quality are not fully reliable and that a human evaluation is always needed.

[3] http://kilgray.com/products/memoq

Table 5: METEOR, 100% matches

company in-house translation memory				
feature	SUB	OJ	NJ	NS
prec	0.60	0.63	0.70	0.66
recall	0.67	0.74	0.74	0.71
F1	0.64	0.68	0.72	0.68
METEOR	0.31	0.37	**0.38**	**0.38**
DGT				
prec	0.76	0.93	0.91	0.81
recall	0.78	0.86	0.88	0.85
F1	0.77	0.89	0.89	0.83
METEOR	0.40	0.50	**0.51**	0.45

Table 6: Error examples, Czech → English.

source seg.	Oblast dat může mít libovolný tvar.
reference	The data area may have an arbitrary shape.
generated seg.	Area data may have any shape.

Error analysis Regarding the precision we have analysed some problematic cases. The most common error was when subsegments are combined in the order in which they occur in the segment assuming the same order in a target language, see the Table 6.

We plan to include a phrase assembly technique that would analyse the input noun phrases and test the fluency of their translation by means of the language model. Results that would not pass a threshold will not take part in the final segment combination method. The best evaluation would be extrinsic: to use generated TMs in a process of translation of a set of documents and measure time needed for the translation.

6 Conclusion

We presented two methods JOIN and SUBSTITUTE which generate new segment pairs for any translation memory and input document. Both methods have variants with overlap and adjoint segments. The techniques include linguistically motivated techniques for filtering out phrases, which provide non-fluent output texts in the target language.

We are co-operating with one of major Central-European translation company which provided us with the testing data and we plan to deploy the methods in their translation process within a future project.

Acknowledgments

This work has been partly supported by the Ministry of Education of CR within the LINDAT-Clarin project LM2010013 and by the Grant Agency of CR within the project 15-13277S.

References

Michael Denkowski and Alon Lavie. 2014. Meteor universal: Language specific translation evaluation for any target language. In *Proceedings of the EACL 2014 Workshop on Statistical Machine Translation*.

Alain Désilets, Benoit Farley, M Stojanovic, and G Patenaude. 2008. WeBiText: Building large heterogeneous translation memories from parallel web content. *Proc. of Translating and the Computer*, 30:27–28.

Qin Gao and Stephan Vogel. 2008. Parallel implementations of word alignment tool. In *Software Engineering, Testing, and Quality Assurance for Natural Language Processing*, pages 49–57. Association for Computational Linguistics.

Kenneth Heafield. 2011. Kenlm: Faster and smaller language model queries. In *Proceedings of the Sixth Workshop on Statistical Machine Translation*, pages 187–197. Association for Computational Linguistics.

Miloš Jakubíček, Adam Kilgarriff, Vojtěch Kovář, Pavel Rychlý, Vít Suchomel, et al. 2013. The tenten corpus family. In *Proc. Int. Conf. on Corpus Linguistics*.

Philipp Koehn, Franz Josef Och, and Daniel Marcu. 2003. Statistical phrase-based translation. In *Proceedings of the 2003 Conference of the North American Chapter of the Association for Computational Linguistics on Human Language Technology-Volume 1*, pages 48–54. Association for Computational Linguistics.

Philipp Koehn, Hieu Hoang, Alexandra Birch, Chris Callison-Burch, Marcello Federico, Nicola Bertoldi, Brooke Cowan, Wade Shen, Christine Moran, Richard Zens, et al. 2007. Moses: Open source toolkit for statistical machine translation. In *Proceedings of the 45th Annual Meeting of the ACL on Interactive Poster and Demonstration Sessions*, pages 177–180. Association for Computational Linguistics.

Elliott Macklovitch, Michel Simard, and Philippe Langlais. 2000. TransSearch: A Free Translation Memory on the World Wide Web. In *Proceedings of the Second International Conference on Language Resources and Evaluation, LREC 2000*.

Francisco Nevado, Francisco Casacuberta, and Josu Landa. 2004. Translation memories enrichment by statistical bilingual segmentation. In *Proceedings of the Fourth International Conference on Language Resources and Evaluation, LREC 2004*.

Franz Josef Och and Hermann Ney. 2003. A systematic comparison of various statistical alignment models. *Computational linguistics*, 29(1):19–51.

Emmanuel Planas and Osamu Furuse. 1999. Formalizing translation memories. In *Machine Translation Summit VII*, pages 331–339.

Emmanuel Planas and Osamu Furuse. 2000. Multi-level similar segment matching algorithm for translation memories and example-based machine translation. In *Proceedings of the 18th conference on Computational linguistics-Volume 2*, pages 621–627. Association for Computational Linguistics.

Michel Simard and Philippe Langlais. 2001. Sub-sentential exploitation of translation memories. In *Machine Translation Summit VIII*, pages 335–339.

Ralf Steinberger, Andreas Eisele, Szymon Klocek, Spyridon Pilos, and Patrick Schlüter. 2013. Dgt-tm: A freely available translation memory in 22 languages. *arXiv preprint arXiv:1309.5226*.

Carlos SC Teixeira, 2014. *The Handling of Translation Metadata in Translation Tools*, page 109. Cambridge Scholars Publishing.

Marco Trombetti. 2009. Creating the world's largest translation memory. In *MT Summit*. `http://mymemory.translated.net`.

CATaLog: New Approaches to TM and Post Editing Interfaces

Tapas Nayek[1], Sudip Kumar Naskar[1], Santanu Pal[2], Marcos Zampieri[2,3], Mihaela Vela[2], Josef van Genabith[2,3]
Jadavpur University, India[1]
Saarland University, Germany[2]
German Research Center for Artificial Intelligence (DFKI), Germany[3]
tnk02.05@gmail.com, sudip.naskar@cse.jdvu.ac.in, m.vela@mx.uni-saarland.de
santanu.pal|marcos.zampieri|josef.vangenabith@uni-saarland.de

Abstract

This paper explores a new TM-based CAT tool entitled *CATaLog*. New features have been integrated into the tool which aim to improve post-editing both in terms of performance and productivity. One of the new features of *CATaLog* is a color coding scheme that is based on the similarity between a particular input sentence and the segments retrieved from the TM. This color coding scheme will help translators to identify which part of the sentence is most likely to require post-editing thus demanding minimal effort and increasing productivity. We demonstrate the tool's functionalities using an English - Bengali dataset.

1 Introduction

The use of translation and text processing software is an important part of the translation workflow. Terminology and computer-aided translation tools (CAT) are among the most widely used software that professional translators use on a regular basis to increase their productivity and also improve consistency in translation.

The core component of the vast majority of CAT tools are translation memories (TM). TMs work under the assumption that previously translated segments can serve as good models for new translations, specially when translating technical or domain specific texts. Translators input new texts into the CAT tool and these texts are divided into shorter segments. The TM engine then checks whether there are segments in the memory which are as similar as possible to those from the input text. Every time the software finds a similar segment in the memory, the tool shows it to the translator as a suitable suggestion usually through a graphical interface. In this scenario, translators work as post-editors by correcting retrieved segments suggested by the CAT tool or translating new segments from scratch. This process is done iteratively and every new translation increases the size of the translation memory making it both more useful and more helpful to future translations.

Although in the first place it might sound very simplistic, the process of matching source and target segments, and retrieving translated segments from the TM is far from trivial. To improve the retrieval engines, researchers have been working on different ways of incorporating semantic knowledge, such as paraphrasing (Utiyama et al., 2011; Gupta and Orăsan, 2014; Gupta et al., 2015), as well as syntax (Clark, 2002; Gotti et al., 2005) in this process. Another recent direction that research in CAT tools is taking is the integration of both TM and machine translation (MT) output (He et al., 2010; Kanavos and Kartsaklis, 2010). With the improvement of state-of-the-art MT systems, MT output is no longer used just for *gisting*, it is now being used in real-world translation projects. Taking advantage of these improvements, CAT tools such as MateCat[1], have been integrating MT output along TMs in the list of suitable suggestions (Cettolo et al., 2013).

In this paper we are concerned both with retrieval and with the post-editing interface of TMs. We present a new CAT tool called *CATaLog*[2], which is language pair independent and allows users to upload their own memories in

[1] `www.matecat.com`

[2] The tool will be released as a freeware open-source software. For more information, use the following URL: `http://ttg.uni-saarland.de/software/catalog`

Proceedings of the Workshop on Natural Language Processing for Translation Memories (NLP4TM), pages 36–42,
Hissar, Bulgaria, Sept 2015.

the tool. Examples showing the basic functionalities of *CATaLog* are presented using English - Bengali data.

2 Related Work

CAT tools have become very popular in the translation and localization industries in the last two decades. They are used by many language service providers, freelance translators to improve translation quality and to increase translator's productivity (Lagoudaki, 2008). Although the work presented in this paper focuses on TM, it should also be noted that there were many studies on MT post-editing published in the last few years (Specia, 2011; Green et al., 2013; Green, 2014) and as mentioned in the last section, one of the recent trends is the development of hybrid systems that are able to combine MT with TM output. Therefore work on MT post-editing presents significant overlap with state-of-the-art CAT tools and to what we propose in this paper.

Substantial work have also been carried out on improving translation recommendation systems which recommends post-editors either to use TM output or MT output (He et al., 2010). To achieve good performance with this kind of systems, researchers typically train a binary classifier (e.g., Support Vector Machines) to decide which output (TM or MT) is most suitable to use for post-editing. Work on integrating MT with TM has also been done to make TM output more suitable for post-editing diminishing translators' effort (Kanavos and Kartsaklis, 2010). Another study presented a *Dynamic Translation Memory* which identifies the longest common subsequence in the the closest matching source segment, identifies the corresponding subsequence in its translation, and dynamically adds this source-target phrase pair to the phrase table of a phrase-based ststistical MT (PB-SMT) system (Biçici and Dymetman, 2008).

Simard and Isabelle (2009) reported a work on integration of PB-SMT with TM technology in a CAT environment in which the PB-SMT system exploits the most similar matches by making use of TM-based feature functions. Koehn and Senellart (2010) reported another MT-TM integration strategy where TM is used to retrieve matching source segments and mismatched portions are translated by an SMT system to fill in the gaps.

Even though this paper describes work in progress, our aim is to develop a tool that is as intuitive as possible for end users and this should have direct impact on translators' performance and productivity. In the recent years, several productive studies were also carried out measuring different aspects of the translation process such as cognitive load, effort, time, quality as well as other criteria (Bowker, 2005; O'Brien, 2006; Guerberof, 2009; Plitt and Masselot, 2010; Federico et al., 2012; Guerberof, 2012; Zampieri and Vela, 2014). User studies were taken into account when developing CATaLog as our main motivation is to improve the translation workflow. In this paper, however, we do not yet explore the impact of our tool in the translation process, because the functionalities required for this kind of study are currently under development in CATaLog. Future work aims to investigate the impact of the new features we are proposing on the translator's work.

3 System Description

We demonstrate the functionalities and features of *CATaLog* in an English - Bengali translation task. The TM database consists of English sentences taken from BTEC[3] (Basic Travel Expression Corpus) corpus and their Bengali translations[4]. Unseen input or test segments are provided to the post-editing tool and the tool matches each of the input segments to the most similar segments contained in the TM. TM segments are then ranked according their the similarity to the test sentence using the popular Translation Error Rate (TER) metric (Snover et al., 2009). The top 5 most similar segments are chosen and presented to the translator ordered by their similarity.

One very important aspect of computing similarity is alignment. Each test (input) segment in the source language (SL) is aligned with the reference SL sentences in the TM and each SL sentence in the TM is aligned to its respective translation. From these two sets

[3]BTEC corpus contains tourism-related sentences similar to those that are usually found in phrase books for tourists going abroad

[4]Work in progress.

of alignments we apply a method to find out which parts of the translation are relevant with respect to the test sentence and which are not, i.e., which parts of the TM translation should remain intact after post editing and which portions should be edited. After this process, matched parts and unmatched parts are color-coded for better visualization; matched parts are displayed in green and unmatched parts are displayed in red. The colors help translators to visualize instantaneously how similar are the five suggested segments to the input segment and which one of them requires the least effort to be post-edited.

3.1 Finding Similarity

For finding out the similar and dissimilar parts between the test segment and a matching TM segment, we use TER alignments. TER is an error metric and it gives an edit ratio (often referred to as edit rate or error rate) in terms of how much editing is required to convert a sentence into another with respect to the length of the first sentence. Allowable edit operations include *insert*, *delete*, *substitute* and *shift*. We use the TER metric (using tercom-7.251[5]) to find the edit rate between a test sentence and the TM reference sentences.

Simard and Fujita (2012) first proposed the use of MT evaluation metrics as similarity functions in implementing TM functionality. They experimented with several MT evaluation metrics, viz. BLEU, NIST, Meteor and TER, and studied their behaviors on TM performance. In the TM tool presented here we use TER as the similarity metric as it is very fast and lightweight and it directly mimics the human post-editing effort. Moreover, the tercom-7.251 package also produces the alignments between the sentence pair from which it is very easy to identify which portions in the matching segment match with the input sentence and which portions need to be worked on. Given below are an input sentence, a TM match and the TER alignment between them where C represents a match (shown as the vertical bar '|'), and I, D and S represents the three post-editing actions - insertion, deletion and substitution, respectively.

[5] http://www.cs.umd.edu/ snover/tercom/

Input: we would like a table by the window .

TM Match: we want to have a table near the window .

TER alignment:

"we","we",C,0
"want","",D,0
"to","would",S,0
"have","like",S,0
"a","a",C,0
"table","table",C,0
"near","by",S,0
"the","the",C,0
"window","window",C,0
".",".",C,0

we	want	to	have	a	table	near	the	window	.
|	D	S	S	|	|	S	|	|	|
we	-	would	like	a	table	by	the	window	.

Since we want to rank reference sentences based on their similarity with the test sentence, we use the TER score in an inverse way. TER being an error metric, the TER score is proportional to how dissimilar two sentences are; i.e., the lower the TER score, the higher the similarity. We can directly use the TER score for ranking of sentences. However, in our present system we have used our own scoring mechanism based on the alignments provided by TER. TER gives equal weight to each edit operation, i.e., deletion, insertion, substitution and shift. However, in post-editing, deletion takes much lesser time compared to the other editing operations. Different costs for different edit operations should yield in better results. These edit costs or weights can be adjusted to get better output from TM. In the present system, we assigned a very low weight to delete operations and equal weights to the other three edit operations. To illustrate why different editing costs matter, let us consider the example below.

- **Test segment:** how much does it cost ?
- **TM segment 1:** how much does it cost to the holiday inn by taxi ?
- **TM segment 2:** how much ?

If each edit operation is assigned an equal weight, according to TER score, TM segment

2 would be a better match with respect to the test segment, as TM segment 2 involves inserting translations for 3 non-matching words in the test segment ("does it cost"), as opposed to deleting translations for 6 non-matching words ("to the holiday inn by taxi") in case of TM segment 1. However, deletion of translations for the 6 non-matching words from the translation of TM segment 1, which are already highlighted red by the TM, takes much less cognitive effort and time than inserting translations of 3 non-matching words into the translation of TM segment 1 in this case. This justifies assigning minimal weights to the deletion operation which prefers TM segment 1 over TM segment 2 for the test segment shown above.

3.2 Color Coding

Among the top 5 choices, post-editor selects one reference translation to do the post-editing task. To make that decision process easy, we color code the matched parts and unmatched parts in each reference translation. Green portion implies that they are matched fragments and red portion implies a mismatch.

The alignments between the TM source sentences and their corresponding translations are generated using GIZA++ (Och and Ney, 2003) in the present work. However, any other word aligner, e.g., Berkley Aligner (Liang et al., 2006), could be used to produce this alignment. The alignment between the matched source segment and the corresponding translation, together with the TER alignment between the input sentence and the matched source segment, are used to generate the aforementioned color coding between selected source and target sentences. The GIZA++ alignment file is directly fed into the present TM tool. Given below is an example TM sentence pair along with the corresponding word alignment input to the TM.

- **English:** we want to have a table near the window .
- **Bengali:** আমরা জানালার কাছে একটা টেবিল চাই ।
- **Alignment:** NUL ({}) we ({ 1 }) want ({ 6 }) to ({ }) have ({ }) a ({ 4 }) table ({ 5 }) near ({ 3 }) the ({ }) window ({ 2 }) . ({ 7 })

GIZA++ generates the alignment between TM source sentences and target sentences. This alignment file is generated offline, only once, on the TM database. TER gives us the alignments between a test sentence and the corresponding top 5 matching sentences. Using these two sets of alignments we color the matched fragments in green and the unmatched fragments in red of the selected source sentences and their corresponding translations.

Color coding the TM source sentences makes explicit which portions of matching TM source sentences match with the test sentence and which ones not. Similarly, color coding the TM target sentences serves two purposes. Firstly, it makes the decision process easier for the translators as to which TM match to choose and work on depending on the color code ratio. Secondly, it guides the translators as to which fragments to post-edit. The reason behind color coding both the TM source and target segments is that a longer (matched or non-matched) source fragment might correspond to a shorter source fragment, or vice versa, due to language divergence. A reference translation which has more green fragments than red fragments will be a good candidate for post-editing. Sometimes smaller sentences may get near 100% green color, but they are not good candidate for post-editing, since post-editors might have to insert translations for more non-matched words in the input sentence. In this context, it is to be noted that insertion and substitution are the most costly operations in post-editing. However, such sentences will not be preferred by the TM as we assign a higher cost for insertion than deletion, and hence such sentences will not be shown as the top candidates by the TM. Figure 1 presents a snapshot of CATaLog.

Input: you gave me wrong number .

Source Matches:

1. you gave me the wrong change . i paid eighty dollars .
2. i think you 've got the wrong number .
3. you are wrong .
4. you pay me .

5. you 're overcharging me .

Target Matches:

1. আপনি আমাকে ভুল খুচরো দিয়েছেন . আমি আশি ডলার দিয়েছি . (*Gloss: apni amake vul khuchro diyechen . ami ashi dollar diyechi .*)
2. আমার ধারণা আপনি ভুল নম্বরে ফোন করেছেন . (*Gloss: amar dharona apni vul nombore phon korechen .*)
3. আপনি ভুল . (*Gloss: apni vul .*)
4. আপনি আমাকে টাকা দিন . (*Gloss: apni amake taka din .*)
5. আপনি আমার কাছে থেকে বেশি নিচ্ছেন . (*Gloss: apni amar kache theke beshi nichchen .*)

For the input sentence shown above, the TM system shows the above mentioned color coded 5 topmost TM matches in order of their relevance with respect to the post-editing effort (as deemed by the TM) for producing the translation for the input sentence.

3.3 Improving Search Efficiency

Comparing every input sentence against all the TM source segments makes the TM very slow. In practical scenario, in order to get good results from a TM, the TM database should be as large as possible. In that case determining the TER alignments will take a lot time for all the reference sentences (i.e., source TM segments). For improving the search efficiency, we make use of the concept of posting lists which is a de facto standard in information retrieval using inverted index.

We create a (source) vocabulary list on the training TM data after removing stop words and other tokens which occur very frequently and have less importance in determining similarity. All the words are then lowercased. Unlike in information retrieval, we do not perform any stemming of the words as we want to store the words in their surface form so that if they appear in the same form as in some input sentence, only then we will consider it as a match. For each word in the vocabulary we maintain a posting list of sentences which contain that word.

We only consider those TM source sentences for similarity measurement which contain one or more vocabulary word(s) of the input sentence. This reduces the search space and the time taken to produce the TM output. The CATaLog tool provides an option whether to use these postings lists or not. This feature is there to compare results using and without using postings lists. In ideal scenario, TM output for both should be the same, though time taken to produce the output will be significantly different.

3.4 Batch Translation

The tool also provides an option for translating sentences in bulk mode. Post-editors can generate TM output for an entire input file at a time using this option. In this case the TM output is saved in a log file which the post-editors can directly work with later in offline mode, i.e., without using the TM tool.

4 Conclusions and Future Work

This paper presents ongoing research and development of a new TM-based CAT tool and post-editing interface entitled *CATaLog*. Even though it describes work in progress, we believe some interesting new insights are discussed and presented in this paper. The tool will be made available in the upcoming months as an open-source free software.

We are currently working on different features to measure time and cognitive load in the post-editing process. The popular keystroke logging is among them. We would like to investigate the impact of the innovations presented here in real world experimental settings with human translators.

We are integrating and refining a couple of features in the tool as for example sentence and clause segmentation using comma and semi-colon as good indicators. It should also be noted that in this paper we considered only word alignments. In the future we would also like to explore how multi-word expressions (MWE) and named entities (NE) can help in TM retrieval and post editing.

We are also exploring contextual, syntactic and semantic features which can be included in similarity scores calculation to retrieve more appropriate translations. Another improvement we are currently working on concerns weight assignment to different edit operations.

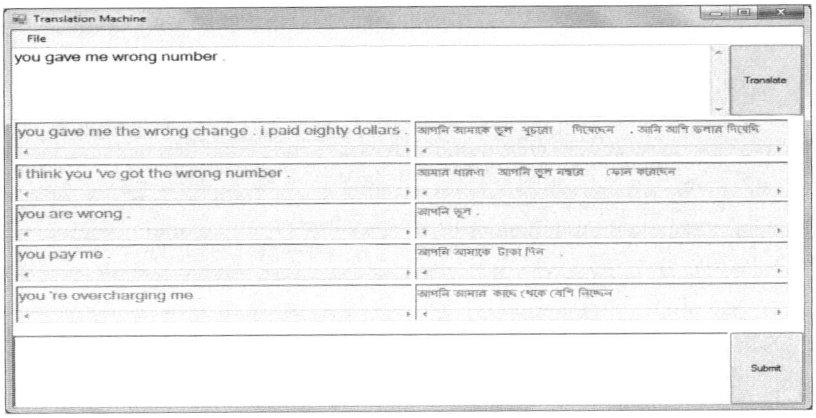

Figure 1: Screenshot with color cording scheme.

We believe these weights can be used to optimize system performance.

Finally, another feature that we are investing is named entity tagging. Named entity lists and gazetteers can be used to identify and to translate named entities in the input text. This will help reduce the translation time and effort for post-editors. The last two improvements we mentioned are, of course, language dependent.

Acknowledgements

We would like to thank the anonymous NLP4TM reviewers who provided us valuable feedback to improve this paper as well as new ideas for future work.

English to Indian language Machine Translation (EILMT) is a project funded by the Department of Information and Technology (DIT), Government of India.

Santanu Pal is supported by the People Programme (Marie Curie Actions) of the European Union's Framework Programme (FP7/2007-2013) under REA grant agreement no 317471.

References

Ergun Biçici and Marc Dymetman. 2008. Dynamic translation memory: using statistical machine translation to improve translation memory fuzzy matches. In *Computational Linguistics and Intelligent Text Processing*, pages 454–465. Springer.

Lynne Bowker. 2005. Productivity vs Quality? A pilot study on the impact of translation memory systems. *Localisation Reader*, pages 133–140.

Mauro Cettolo, Christophe Servan, Nicola Bertoldi, Marcello Federico, Loic Barrault, and Holger Schwenk. 2013. Issues in incremental adaptation of statistical MT from human post-edits. In *Proceedings of the Workshop on Post-editing Technology and Practice (WPTP-2)*, Nice, France.

J.P. Clark. 2002. System, method, and product for dynamically aligning translations in a translation-memory system, February 5. US Patent 6,345,244.

Marcello Federico, Alessandro Cattelan, and Marco Trombetti. 2012. Measuring User Productivity in Machine Translation Enhanced Computer Assisted Translation. In *Proceedings of Conference of the Association for Machine Translation in the Americas (AMTA)*.

Fabrizio Gotti, Philippe Langlais, Elliott Macklovitch, Benoit Robichaud Didier Bourigault, and Claude Coulombe. 2005. 3GTM: A Third-Generation Translation Memory. In *3rd Computational Linguistics in the North-East (CLiNE) Workshop*, Gatineau, Québec, aug.

Spence Green, Jeffrey Heer, and Christopher D Manning. 2013. The efficacy of human post-editing for language translation. In *Proceedings of the SIGCHI Conference on Human Factors in Computing Systems*.

Spence Green. 2014. *Mixed-initiative natural language translation*. Ph.D. thesis, Stanford University.

Ana Guerberof. 2009. Productivity and quality in the post-editing of outputs from translation memories and machine translation. *Localisation Focus*, 7(1):133–140.

Ana Guerberof. 2012. *Productivity and Quality in the Post-Edition of Outputs from Translation Memories and Machine Translation*. Ph.D. thesis, Rovira and Virgili University Tarragona.

Rohit Gupta and Constantin Orăsan. 2014. Incorporating Paraphrasing in Translation Memory Matching and Retrieval. In *Proceedings of EAMT.*

Rohit Gupta, Constantin Orăsan, Marcos Zampieri, Mihaela Vela, and Josef van Genabith. 2015. Can Translation Memories afford not to use paraphrasing? In *Proceedings of EAMT.*

Yifan He, Yanjun Ma, Josef van Genabith, and Andy Way. 2010. Bridging SMT and TM with translation recommendation. In *Proceedings of ACL*, pages 622–630.

Panagiotis Kanavos and Dimitrios Kartsaklis. 2010. Integrating Machine Translation with Translation Memory: A Practical Approach. In *Proceedings of the Second Joint EM+/CNGL Workshop Bringing MT to the User: Research on Integrating MT in the Translation Industry.*

Philipp Koehn and Jean Senellart. 2010. Convergence of translation memory and statistical machine translation. In *Proceedings of AMTA Workshop on MT Research and the Translation Industry*, pages 21–31.

Elina Lagoudaki. 2008. The value of machine translation for the professional translator. In *Proceedings of the 8th Conference of the Association for Machine Translation in the Americas*, pages 262–269, Waikiki, Hawaii.

Percy Liang, Ben Taskar, and Dan Klein. 2006. Alignment by Agreement. In *Proceedings of the Main Conference on Human Language Technology Conference of the North American Chapter of the Association of Computational Linguistics*, pages 104–111.

Sharon O'Brien. 2006. Eye-tracking and translation memory matches. *Perspectives: Studies in Translatology*, 14:185–204.

Franz Josef Och and Hermann Ney. 2003. A systematic comparison of various statistical alignment models. *Computational linguistics*, 29(1):19–51.

Mirko Plitt and François Masselot. 2010. A productivity test of statistical machine translation post-editing in a typical localisation context. *The Prague Bulletin of Mathematical Linguistics*, 93:7–16.

Michel Simard and Atsushi Fujita. 2012. A Poor Man's Translation Memory Using Machine Translation Evaluation Metrics. In *Proceedings of the 10th Biennial Conference of the Association for Machine Translation in the Americas (AMTA)*, San Diego, California, USA.

Michel Simard and Pierre Isabelle. 2009. Phrase-based machine translation in a computer-assisted translation environment. *Proceedings of the Twelfth Machine Translation Summit (MT Summit XII)*, pages 120–127.

Matthew Snover, Nitin Madnani, Bonnie Dorr, and Richard Schwartz. 2009. Fluency, Adequacy, or HTER? Exploring Different Human Judgments with a Tunable MT Metric. In *Proceedings of the Fourth Workshop on Statistical Machine Translation*, EACL 2009.

Lucia Specia. 2011. Exploiting objective annotations for measuring translation post-editing effort. In *Proceedings of the 15th Conference of the European Association for Machine Translation*, pages 73–80, Leuven, Belgium.

Masao Utiyama, Graham Neubig, Takashi Onishi, and Eiichiro Sumita. 2011. Searching Translation Memories for Paraphrases. pages 325–331.

Marcos Zampieri and Mihaela Vela. 2014. Quantifying the Influence of MT Output in the Translators' Performance: A Case Study in Technical Translation. In *Proceedings of the Workshop on Humans and Computer-assisted Translation (HaCaT 2014).*

Author Index